THE POLITICS OF FINANCIAL CONTROL

Politics

Editor

PROFESSOR W. A. ROBSON
Professor Emeritus of Public Administration
in the University of London

THE POLITICS OF
FINANCIAL CONTROL

THE ROLE OF THE HOUSE OF COMMONS

Gordon Reid
Professor of Politics in the
University of Western Australia

HUTCHINSON UNIVERSITY LIBRARY
LONDON

HUTCHINSON & CO (*Publishers*) LTD
178–202 Great Portland Street, London W1

London Melbourne Sydney
Auckland Bombay Toronto
Johannesburg New York

★

First published 1966

*This book has been set in Bembo, printed in Great Britain
on Smooth Wove paper by Anchor Press, and
bound by Wm. Brendon, both of Tiptree, Essex*

CONTENTS

Preface   7

1 The mysteries of parliamentary financial procedure   9

2 Campion's four rules of financial procedure   33

3 The control of expenditure by parliamentary debate   62

4 The financial select committees   93

5 Raising the revenue   127

6 Is parliamentary financial control a myth?   146

Select Bibliography   165

Index   173

PREFACE

This is a book about an ancient and important function of Britain's House of Commons, viz. the control of finance—or what is popularly known as 'The Control of the Purse'. It follows a long line of books on the same subject, many of them written by illustrious authorities on the British Constitutions. The sole explanation I offer for having the temerity to add yet another title is simply that I find the existing books to be deficient. To me, they fail to give a complete understanding of *why* the House of Commons does what it does in the performance of its financial functions. My hope, then, is that this short, unorthodox, treatment of the subject might help to overcome that deficiency, if in fact it exists.

The book is not meant to be the last word on parliamentary control of finance. The subject is far too complex, and imporant, to be disposed of within its short compass. Indeed, I hope it provokes more questions than it answers, particularly questions about the role of representative assemblies in modern industrial societies, and about the process I call 'parliamentary politics'.

My thanks for the opportunity to write the book go to the Trustees of the Nuffield Foundation who awarded me a Nuffield Dominion Travelling Fellowship in the humanities, which permitted me to work in London during that memorable year of political crises—1963. I also thank the University of Adelaide for granting me leave to take up the Nuffield award.

I was fortunate that most of the research for the book could be done under one roof. I had access to the extensive resources of the British Library of Political and Economic Science at the London School of Economics. My gratitude and admiration go out to that library's staff. Within the LSE I have personal debts to many people. In particular it was the late Professor Reg Bassett who originally encouraged me to work in this field. His enthusiasm for the study of Parliament was infectious. I suspect he would have disagreed with many of my conclusions but I know they would have benefited from his criticism. In addition, Professor Michael Oakeshott and Dr Anne Bohm smoothed a path for me in innumerable and kindly ways. My debt to them is great. But in no sense should any of the criticism the book earns rub off on to them.

I must acknowledge the kindness I received at the hands of officials of British government—at the Treasury and at the House of Commons. In both places I found constant, sympathetic help and a tolerance of ignorance that facilitated my work at the expense of theirs. I know the officials concerned would prefer to remain anonymous, so in deference to their philosophy, I emphasise my gratitude to them rather than their names.

My ex-colleagues in the Department of Politics at the University of Adelaide listened to my exposition of the ideas in this book with infinite patience and they commented critically and constructively on them. In many respects the ideas took their final shape in the academic environment they created. But, notwithstanding my indebtedness to them, the book is completely my own responsibility.

And finally, for the typing of the manuscript, I am particularly grateful to Mrs Gwen Rice and Mrs Joan Middleton of the University of Adelaide.

I

THE MYSTERIES OF
PARLIAMENTARY FINANCIAL PROCEDURE

'Parliamentary Control of the Purse' is held to be a basic principle of the British Constitution; and, *ipso facto*, a similar significance is claimed for it in the many nations that have Constitutions modelled on Whitehall-Westminster relationships. But in modern industrialised societies the expression is an enigma. It accords with the aspirations of most elected representatives to restrain excesses of Executive authority, and it bolsters their social and political status. But at the same time, with public expenditure totalling thousands of millions of pounds annually (in excess of £7,000 millions in Britain in 1966), and with financial policies of government now affecting every member of the community, a literal application of the principle would constitute a threat to prompt, positive and consistent decision-making in government. What, therefore, does the expression mean in modern economic conditions? And, more particularly, what does it mean in British government today?

A study of parliamentary control of finance in Britain brings a focus of interest upon the elected House—the House of Commons. The Parliament Act 1911, amongst other things, gives legal expression to that House's financial superiority. Although it is not financially all-embracive, applying strictly to proposed laws that comply with its definition of a 'money bill', that Act is a legal epitome of the financial ascendancy that the Commons House has achieved.

In the existing political-financial relationships in Parliament the House of Lords counts for little; indeed, it will scarcely be mentioned below.

The methods of parliamentary financial control as pursued in Britain are notoriously confusing. Gladstone's famous financial reforms of a century ago, which remain the basis of contemporary arrangements, presuppose that the House of Commons exercises an infinite control in finance analogous to that a person may hold over a mechanical device such as an automobile or an aircraft. The House's financial procedures, both for revenue and taxation business, are expressions of its aspirations to financial power; they are legislative procedures, and they presume that the elective body, in the cause of economy in government, may make both quantitative and qualitative alterations to the Executive's financial plans, and thus contribute directly to the process of policy determination. Their authority is enhanced and perpetuated by the House's historic but sporadic claims to change policy or to invoke a veto over any financial proposal put to it. Their fundamental premise is that representative assent to all taxation, and to all public expenditure, is basic to British democracy.

However, as a result of the emergence since Gladstone of mass, disciplined, and nationally based political parties, financial control has gained a new connotation. In consequence of the strict party-allegiances of the membership of the House, and the reluctance of any one party to yield openly to the pressures of another, 'control' has gradually taken the meaning of the French *contrôler* and gives rise to an interpretation of the House's financial function as being to check, to supervise, to verify, or to safeguard the finances of the State. The House, it is said, has no direct role in financial-policy decisions but simply discusses, formally legitimises, and, with the assistance of a Comptroller and Auditor-General and its own select committees, reviews financial decisions and financial allocations that are agreed upon elsewhere.

In reality, and adding to the confusion, neither of these interpretations wholly accords with the facts. Although the House spends most of its time on financial issues in broad and general debate, and exercises a modicum of review and supervision through its financial select committees, it does in some subjects, for example taxation, continue to use its legislative power and shape the expression of revenue policy in law. Pressure groups, to their satisfaction, still find MP's capable of influencing taxation law during the parliamentary process. But the very same parliamentarians are barren when it comes to a similar influence in the parliamentary approval of the annual expenditure plans. The House's differential treatment of the categories of its financial business encourages closer examination.

The author has been attracted to this field of enquiry as a result of the use of the so-called 'Westminster model' overseas—particularly in Australia—and the difficulties encountered there in adapting traditional parliamentary methods, emergent from English political life, in a representative institution belonging to a new and different social environment. The Australian House of Representatives on May Day 1963, after sixty-two years of confused application and misunderstanding, abolished much of the ancient financial paraphernalia and the mysterious jargon of financial control it inherited from the Imperial Parliament. But with that abolition have gone many of the parliamentary aspirations in finance that the Imperial procedures symbolised. And now, bereft of the ancient forms, the procedures remaining illustrate in stark relief a brute authority that the Executive wields in finance over the lower House. The subsequent developments in Australia will be interesting, but they are for another study. Here it is necessary to ask whether similar reforms in the United Kingdom, which have been suggested in the House of Commons, would have similar effect.

In Britain substantial changes have already been made in the wider field of public finance. As the result of extensive enquiries and the recommendations of bodies such as the Estimates Committee of the House of Commons (particularly its report on Treasury Control),[1] the Crick Committee on 'The Form of Public Accounts',[2] the Plowden Committee on 'Control of Public Expenditure',[3] and the

1. H C 254-1 (Session 1957-8).   2. Cmd 7969.   3. Cmnd 1432.

departmental report on 'Reform of the Exchequer Accounts',[1] much
has been achieved. The reports published so far have provided
welcome information about the changing financial-administrative
process. But, significantly, the reforms emerging have concentrated on the financial practices of the Executive, particularly the
Treasury, and its control of departmental expenditure and accounting arrangements. Parliamentary aims and methods have been
treated as sacred territory and excluded, by direction or by implica-
tion, from the terms of reference of the enquiring bodies. . . . 'It is
incumbent upon us', reported the Crick Committee in 1950, 'to
refrain from making proposals which might impair at any point the
efficacy of Parliamentary control, as at present operative, over
expenditure and the raising of money.'[2] And the Plowden Committee in 1961, in its report entitled 'Control of Public Expenditure',
explained: 'We have not sought to go deeply into the relations
between Parliament and the Executive in the control of expenditure,
or the procedures by which Parliament debates and authorises
supply.'[3] All the above Committees proceeded in their enquiries
with any latent reforming zeal for parliamentary control firmly
restrained.

The preclusion of official enquiries from matters of parliamentary
procedure is, however, defensible. If parliamentary sovereignty
means anything it means the privilege that members have to
determine collectively the procedures for their respective Houses:
it is unlikely to be delegated. But that does not justify the absence
in the House of Commons of attempts to effect with the Executive
a co-ordinated review of financial arrangements. Perhaps parliamentary sovereignty should promote parliamentary initiative in
reform; and with the growing complexities of government, the
necessity for this in matters of finance would seem to be increasing.
But there are fears of change, and restraints upon it. It is significant
that when a House of Commons' Select Committee on Procedure
in 1948 was faced with the need for providing a complete understanding and a possible redefinition of the House's financial methods,

1. Cmnd 2014.   Cmd 7969, p. 12.   3. Cmnd 1432, p. 21.

it retreated from its task. The explanation was: 'While Your Committee recognise that the Standing Orders relating to Public Money some of which are of considerable antiquity, afford a very inadequate expression of modern practice, they have . . . left them untouched, since their revision would require special technical knowledge and involve labour and research for which the time is not at present available. Your Committee suggest that attention might be given to this matter at some future time.'[1] There is no indication that the required 'attention' has been given them since. The Standing Orders in question include some of late seventeenth- and early eighteenth-century origin, and they are considered fundamental to the whole financial process. Presumably, without the requisite 'technical knowledge' for their revision, they continue to be applied in a political and economic context quite unrelated to the circumstances of their origin. Their antiquity undoubtedly has evoked profound respect, even awe, from parliamentary observers and participants alike. Indeed, over the centuries they have become enveloped in innumerable procedural 'rulings' and 'precedents' and also a technical jargon, all of which has produced a curious mystique. The financial procedures of the House are fully comprehensible only to the few who work closest to them. Before attempting to make an outsider's evaluation of them, therefore (or for that matter any rule of procedure—ancient or modern), consideration should be given to the wider procedural corpus to which they belong.

'Procedure', the dictionaries say, is the 'mode of conducting business'. Assuming the acceptability of this, our interest is in the mode of conduct in one section—the financial—of the business of the House of Commons. If representative institutions are essential to democracy—as an integral part of the process of counting heads in preference to breaking them—then the methods chosen by elected members for discussion in them have no small democratic significance. And there is no reason why discussions in finance should be any less important.

'There is nothing which is peculiar in the procedural rules of a

1. H C 192 (Session 1947–8), p. iii.

representative parliament,' wrote Sir Ernest Barker. 'Every public meeting, every local council, and every voluntary association has its standing orders, which (since such bodies are analogous to parliaments) are similar to the standing orders and procedural rules of parliaments. With the passage of time the procedural rules of all these bodies harden, and they also multiply.'[1] While this explains procedures simply, it detracts some importance from the debating rules of the nation's principal representative body. For in that context the rules control the discussion of, and in many respects the decision-making for, national rather than local issues. They are the formal means for the institutional approval of national political ends, for the conflict of political ideas in a national political forum, and, in theory, they guide the activity of open political compromise in national government. Democrats ignore them at their peril.

In all formal deliberation procedural rules are essential to the attainment of any semblance of ordered progress. Their importance to the judicial process is, for example, universally recognised and procedural wrangling has become an interesting and significant prelude to international and summit conferences. 'Without rules', said Bentham (in advising the French on parliamentary tactics), 'the power of the Assembly either evaporates in ineffectual struggles, or becomes a prey to the obstinate and overbearing.'[2] And before Bentham wrote, the Clerk of the House of Commons (John Hatsell, about 1776) made his notorious comment that 'it is more material that there should be a rule to go by than what the rule is.'[3] These men feared that unrestrained parliamentary oratory invited demagogy. For them, anything was better than anarchy. But their procedural prescriptions proved inadequate to representative democracy; they discounted the qualitative elements of procedural rules.

It is not difficult today to envisage, and even to observe, how the power of an assembly may be 'evaporated' by rules; and how the

1. Sir E. Barker, *Reflections on Government* (O U P, 1942), p. 208.

2. Jeremy Bentham, *Essay on Political Tactics* in *The Works of Jeremy Bentham*, ed. John Bowring (Tait, 1843), vol II, p. 332.

3. Quoted in Erskine May, *Parliamentary Practice* (sixteenth edition), p. xlix.

'obstinate and overbearing' may gain their ascendancy through rules. Rules for a deliberative process have either a positive or a negative effect, providing rights or limiting opportunities. Moreover, they can mask reality. Just as the formal shape of an organisation may differ from its true outlines, or as the legal provisions of a Constitution may not explain its social implications, so parliamentary rules of procedure may differ in form and in practice. They have to be studied in the light of their effect as well as from the viewpoint of their origin and expression.

The House of Commons, in keeping with the society it serves, is renowned for its retention of ancient ways. Tradition is its daily bread. Its procedural peculiarities are usually explained in terms of social or institutional nostalgia, or, as Josef Redlich once put it, they are an expression of 'constructive conservatism'.[1] There is a multiplicity of procedural forms, ancient in their origin, constantly being adapted in matters of detail, to changing political needs, but always claiming a firm foundation in the past. At any time the description of a particular branch of its procedure is long and historically involved.

But 'conservatism', 'institutional nostalgia' or even 'traditionalism', may not be the only, or even the prime, criteria of the House's procedural determinations. The House does not live by traditional bread alone. There are other reasons for the preservation of methods of the past. Walter Bagehot, as was his *forte*, went deeper in analysis. 'It is the dull traditional habit of mankind that guides most men's actions. . . . Other things being equal, yesterday's institutions are by far the best for today; they are the most ready, the most influential, the most easy to get obeyed. . . .'[2] And it is here that Bagehot suggests the direction of our enquiry. Behind yesterday's institutions may live today's power. Some of the financial procedures, in spite of their antiquity, may still be sources of power and influence in a political assembly, and as such they could be factors of no mean

1. Josef Redlich, *The Procedure of the House of Commons* (Constable, 1908), vol III, p. 161.
2. Walter Bagehot, *The English Constitution* (Fontana Library edition, 1963), pp. 64–5.

political priority. The truth could be lost if we dismiss them as merely 'traditional'; or, in fits of reform, simply claim that they are irrelevant to the needs of the day; or if we blandly classify them with Bagehot's 'dignified' parts of the Constitution—as being 'very complicated, and somewhat imposing, very old and rather venerable'.[1] It is necessary in evaluating parliamentary procedures —old or new—to measure their political utility.

Although adopted in one political circumstance, a rule of deliberation can be retained and used in another with a differing result. 'Much ingenuity', claimed a Clerk of the House of Commons (Sir Courtenay Ilbert), 'has been shown in adapting them [the rules] to the circumstances and requirements of the time.'[2] Ingenuity, of course, knows many motives. Rules formulated in the seventeenth century to assist the House's control of the King's profligacy (i.e. for the Committee of the Whole House) may be 'adapted' in the twentieth century to subordinate a democratically elected assembly to the Executive's will. Rules formulated in the nineteenth century to facilitate debate and to promote economy in governmental expenditure (i.e. for granting Estimates) may be used in the twentieth century to shelter a government from the free flow of political ideas. The purpose in this study is to give first priority to what particular rules achieve in the deliberative process rather than what they represent historically. When rules are retained in an institution on the ground of being ancient there is cause for questioning. And in no part of the House of Commons' procedures are there methods more ancient in their origin than in that part related to financial business.

But what are procedural rules, and how are they made? It is well known that in the House of Commons there is no comprehensive written code of procedure to define its behaviour. Its procedural rules are a complex blend of parliamentary practice (said to grow out of precedent), declared Standing Orders, and enacted law. But on all matters procedural the House is held to be supreme. 'Freedom

1. *ibid*, p. 65.
2. Redlich, *op. cit.* (preface by Sir Courtenay Ilbert), vol I, p. vi.

of speech and debates or proceedings in Parliament', says the Bill of Rights, 'ought not to be impeached or questioned in any Court or Place outside of Parliament.' And Blackstone made it clear that each House of Parliament takes this right to itself and, procedurally, is beyond judicial restraint.[1] One of the more important outcomes of the physical and legal clashes in the 1880's between Nottingham's Charles Bradlaugh and Westminster's Serjeant-at-Arms, Henry Gossett, was the '. . . unqualified recognition of the courts of their incompetence to enquire into the internal proceedings of a House of Parliament'; and also the declaration of the Chief Justice that where the procedure of a House or the right of its members to take part in its proceedings is dependent on statute the House can 'practically change or practically supersede the law'.[2]

If we acknowledge the theory of the House's procedural autonomy then we must ask whether it—qua House—pursues any consistent philosophy in its rule determination. The House's propensity for retaining methods of the past is not unusual in social institutions. F. M. Cornford in his *Microcosmographia Academica*, for example, warned of a disposition towards conservatism in all social living, including the methods of deliberative bodies: 'Nothing is ever done until everyone is convinced that it ought to be done, and has been convinced for so long that it is now time to do something else.'[3] And about half a century earlier, in 1861, a House of Commons Select Committee on Procedure recommended that the House should pursue a procedural philosophy along those lines—'no change is justifiable which experience has not proved to be necessary, and the maintenance of old rules is preferable to new but speculative amendments.'[4] Indeed, as recently as 1960, the Leader of the House (R. A. Butler), when speaking of financial procedures, warned that 'if we were to depart unduly from these guardrails and these sorts of guides . . . which have guided and looked after the liberties of our

1. *Commentaries on the Law of England* (second edition, OUP), vol I, p. 163.
2. For a summary of *Bradlaugh v. Gossett*, see Erskine May, *Parliamentary Practice* (seventeenth edition, Butterworth, 1964), pp. 60–1.
3. Fifth edition, Bowes and Bowes (1953), p. 2. (First published 1908.)
4. HC 173 (Session 1861), p. 7.

B

ancestors, we should be making a mistake.'[1] Change is at times
acceptable, but there is no precise criterion to indicate when.

The House, therefore, we can say with assurance, is procedurally
conservative. It still wears, as Bagehot claimed of the English
Constitution, 'clothes in the fashion of its youth'. But does this
mean it can be charged with procedural dilatoriness? Such a conclusion might be drawn from Campion's well-known generalisa-
tion 'Parliamentary procedure is always a little out of date',[2] which
is rather like the familiar proposition 'the law is archaic'. Both are
likely to mislead. The preferences that Members of Parliament show
for the methods of the past over 'new but speculative amendments'
do not preclude change, they merely limit it. The methods of the
House are constantly being modified. The successive reports of the
Select Committees on Procedure in the last century manifest a continuing procedural introspection by members. The House has not
been dilatory. Changes have been frequent. But they have also been
gradual, not radical. What is significant, and Campion's statement
does not acknowledge it, is that along with the gradualness of the
change in these days of radical social reform, and with the House's
failure to engage in root and branch procedural reform, the Executive has assumed its present dominant hold over Parliament. And this
situation has been abetted by the tendency in the affairs of the House
to inflate statements such as Campion's into procedural prescriptions.

It is the observance of the maxim of adherence to procedural
precedent that does most to bolster conservatism in the methods of
the House. In some respects there is an attitude of immutability.
Around fundamental and ancient practices, and around the modern
Standing Orders, particularly in relation to financial business, there
is an accumulation of rulings from the Chair, often referred to as
the 'case-law' of the House; and this, like Common Law, is built on
the application of old principles to new conditions. It involves the
control of the present by the wisdom of the past, and it accords
with Burke's '. . . neither *now* nor at *any* time, is it prudent or safe

1. 617 HC Deb., 5s., c. 44.   2. HC 189-1 (Session 1945-6), p. v.

to be meddling with the fundamental principles and ancient usage of our constitution. . . .'[1] Burke's ghost lingers on. 'It would be quite impossible', said the House's Deputy Speaker on a financial issue in 1961, 'that I should be invited to reverse a ruling of my predecessor.'[2] Whilst that is comforting to people of conservative disposition, it cannot always prevail. There develops, as Lord Tennyson noted:

> That codeless myriad of precedent
> That wilderness of single instances.[3]

The procedures of the House are not as inflexible as some of its pedants assert. In the modern state, absolute adherence to precedent is virtually impossible; it would tend to bring parliamentary business to a standstill. For in addition to new types of business there are innumerable situations, and altered values in political behaviour, that demand procedural change. And just as judges purge their own doctrine, so the House purges its own precedent. Just as precedent was rejected with the introduction of the closure procedure in 1882, so it was rejected in 1963 when the House was adjourned as a mark of respect upon the death of the Leader of the Opposition (Mr Gaitskell). Then the Prime Minister (Mr Macmillan) explained: 'I have felt in matters of this kind precedents should be regarded as a general guide and not as rules to be adhered to pedantically and slavishly.'[4] The occasion was sorrowful but the change was possible, as it is always possible, if it is in accord with the so-called 'sense of the House' or what might be called the 'general will' of parliamentary behaviour. The determinants of the House's 'sense' or of its 'general will' are often vague and imprecise, but at this point it should be noted that procedures are not immutable, and that precedents are binding in the House only for as long as the balance of power for the time being in procedural affairs is

---

1. Edmund Burke, Speech to the House of Commons, 7 May 1782. See *Works* (F. and J. Revington, 1852), vol VI, p. 128.
2. 635 H C Deb., 5s., cc. 250–1.   3. 'Aylmers Field.'
4. 670 H C Deb., 5s., c. 40.

agreed that they should be binding. 'Adherence to precedent', therefore, is a useful parliamentary commandment. It is preached in the interests of procedural stability, and, not the least, by the occupant of the Chair.

The Standing Orders of the House are manifestations of procedural change. They have been found necessary from time to time to effect declared alterations to what were deemed ancient practices. They are simply procedural resolutions of the House deemed to have permanent validity. Lord Campion pointed out they '. . . are not in any sense a code, but everywhere assume a settled practice which they modify only in detail'.[1] There are at present 117 of them, but some are long and involved fiats that in other legislatures would gain expression in multiple orders. Three of them (at present Nos. 82, 83, and 85) found their first expression in Standing Orders early in the eighteenth century—these are the ancient 'Public Money' Orders which have been retained for purposes to be described below; and, as we shall see, they too have been altered, if not in the letter, then in their interpretation.

The remaining 114 Standing Orders are, significantly, of post-1832 origin, and their purpose and effect cannot be isolated from the need to control the House's changing deliberative climate in the wake of the franchise reform of the late-nineteenth and early-twentieth centuries. Ironically, the coming of representative democracy has been paralleled by the introduction of restrictive and, in some respects, repressive debating rules.

On the whole the Standing Orders are instruments of control. Some people may say control of debate, or of the use of the time of the House, but in this study they will be considered to exist for the control of politics in the representative assembly—assuming that politics is the activity by which diverse interests contend, conflict and are resolved. The Standing Orders have been frequently altered, simply by resolution of the House, sometimes in relaxation of the restrictions they impose but more frequently in their intensifica-

---

1. Lord Campion, G CB, *An Introduction to the Procedure of the House of Commons* (third edition, Macmillan, 1958), p. 2.

tion. The acceptance of the House of 114 Orders in 130 years, especially when we recognise some of their provisions, is not procedural immobility, nor is it dilatoriness. But changes have always been piecemeal. The Standing Orders are the result of a process of evolution, there has been no procedural revolution and no fresh start.

There is a third category of procedure that has particular financial relevance—namely, statute. The procedural autonomy of each House means that neither can interfere with the processes of the other. The sensitivity of members in inter-House relationships is notorious and conflicts have left their marks on British parliamentary history. For example, the widely known Parliament Act 1911, declaring inter-House financial relationships, can be seen as a justiciable solution to what was a continuing political-procedural problem. It settled a long-standing dispute with relative finality. In other cases statutes have declared the financial methods of the Commons alone. There are, for example, the Public Accounts and Charges Act 1891 and the Provisional Collection of Taxes Act 1913, providing for the ordinary procedures of law-making to be short-circuited so as to allow particular financial resolutions of the House to have immediate legal effect, subject to conditions, and for a prescribed period. These statutes prescribe procedures, and they have emerged from particular political situations. But even though enshrined in statute such procedures are not immutable. Their peculiarity is that they are less flexible. They may only be changed through a legislative process.[1] That is to say, for procedural changes via statute, the 'sense' of the House has to be measured through the longer process of law making.

Procedure—a House of Commons matter?

As an expression of the House's autonomy in the choice of its debating rules, it is often said that a procedural matter is a 'House of

---

1. It is pointed out in *Bradlaugh v. Gossett* (12 QBD, pp. 280–1): 'the House of Commons has exclusive power of interpreting the statute, so far as the regulation of its own proceedings within its own walls is concerned'. And see May, *op. cit.* (seventeenth edition), p. 61.

Commons matter'. 'The subject', claimed a recent study—*What's Wrong with Parliament?*—'is essentially a House one, and one on which Members should come to their own independent conclusions.'[1] It is frequently inferred that in the discussion and the determination of procedural questions members of the House subordinate their party political values to the institutional (or constitutional) importance of the House. Redlich's assessment of procedural development in his time was: 'It is a striking fact that amendment of procedure was, almost from beginning to end, treated without party spirit, not as an issue between two great parties but as a problem for the House of Commons as a whole.'[2] Possibly that conclusion could be justified in the nineteenth century, but its application to the twentieth is questionable. Redlich witnessed a greater flexibility—or less discipline—in the party system than we know today. There was a continuing suspicion of governmental procedural motives, and less readiness to yield to front bench attitudes. Governments were obliged to seek wider approval for their reforming proposals and to win the confidence of the House. In the main they used select committees on procedure to search for the elusive consensus. But as techniques of enquiry and agreement the committees were not blessed with success. In 1881 Erskine May considered their work in his lifetime had been 'curiously sterile'.[3] And in 1882 Gladstone despaired of change through them, claiming '. . . there have been more committees of this House upon this subject than upon any other. There have been fourteen committees since the Reform Act.' Their effort, he said, had been a 'total failure'. Eight select committees between 1837 and 1882 considered proposals for the *cloture* but failed to recommend its adoption. That in Gladstone's opinion justified the Government's intervention to provide the 'propelling power' on matters of procedural change. He moved successfully to have the *cloture* procedure permanently adopted and thus marked the beginning of a trend wherein the

1. Andrew Hill and Anthony Whichelow, *What's Wrong with Parliament?* (Penguin Special, 1964), p. 95.
2. Redlich, *op. cit.*, vol I, pp. 125–6.
3. See *Political Tracts* 1819–81 (British Museum).

government of the day took an overt and active interest in the House's procedural machinery.[1]

In 1902, when Mr Balfour (Leader of the House and first Lord of the Treasury) wanted to regulate parliamentary behaviour and the use of parliamentary time along the lines of a railway time-table (and to affirm a number of reforms applied provisionally since 1896), he acted unilaterally. He had the necessary party support for his plans and eschewed select committee preliminaries. On that occasion the Leader of the Opposition (Henry Campbell-Bannerman) claimed that the proposals were 'so grave, so extensive, so far reaching, so heterogeneous, interfering as they do, with the almost immemorial arrangements . . . of this House . . .' they demanded prior select committee approval.[2] But his words were wasted. '. . . no human being', said Balfour (presumably including everyone), 'who has spoken on either side, cares one farthing for a Select Committee.'[3] His party backed him.

In spite of Balfour's attitude it is interesting that in subsequent years select committee enquiries have remained popular instruments for procedural change or procedural politics. But this does not mean that governments have lost the propelling power. Select Committees on Procedure are now used in a variety of ways. The Rt Hon Herbert (later Lord) Morrison, for example, used one in 1945-6 to achieve the reforms he considered necessary to equip the House to handle his party's post-war legislative programme. He submitted his own ideas for reform, spending five days giving evidence. And although that committee looked favourably upon some of his proposals, it rejected others. Morrison argued openly about their rejection, and finally the committee lost. When the question came before the House the Whips were called on and Morrison's proposals were pushed through by force of party numbers. On that occasion an indignant Mr Harold Macmillan on the Opposition side expressed concern. 'I know we shall be voted down because, though this is a House of Commons matter, it has not been left to the House of Commons. Not a single question since we started . . .

1. 266 HC Deb., 3s., c. 1134.   2. 111 HC Deb., 4s., c. 549.   3. *ibid*, c. 774.

has been left to a free vote. The Whips have been put on. . . .'
Macmillan also pointed out: 'These are much more House of Commons matters than matters of the division between the parties—as between who for the moment holds office and who for the moment is in Opposition. But in the mutability of human affairs we must take into account that we may find ourselves in a different position.'[1]

Macmillan's turn came, but his government used the same technique. In 1960, after the extensive enquiries of the 1958-9 Select Committee on Procedure, the Leader of the House (R. A. Butler) was eclectic. He accepted the minor proposals of the committee, but rejected others—including proposals for shifting financial business to standing committees. On that occasion back-benchers on both sides expressed dissatisfaction, especially those who had served on the committee. 'I am shocked', said one from the Opposition side, 'that the Whips have been put on on this occasion . . . there ought to be a free vote because there is nothing political about this; it is a matter which concerns every Hon Member.'[2] But again protests were in vain, and the Government won.

In the House of Commons, in procedural matters, the expression 'There is nothing political about this' is a cry of deception or defeat. How could the procedures of the House be beyond politics? And it is the same with the cry 'This is a House of Commons matter'. It is as much as saying that after their struggle to win the seats of executive power the victors should be neutral in the determination of the controls they may exercise over the institutional source of their authority—the House. Power, for the party in government, is too precious a possession to be left to the four winds of institutional altruism. Nor could it be expected that the party leaders who have lost, or who covet executive power would be unaware of the political significance of parliamentary procedures. But the notion of the House's procedural hegemony dies hard. It is a legacy of the days prior to nationally based political parties when consensus had to be won, not whipped. Governments continue to

1. 443 HC Deb., 5s., cc. 1722-6.
2. F. Blackburn, 617 HC Deb., 5s., c. 60.

give lip-service to it by persisting with select committees on procedural topics, but this is all part of a political process.

It is interesting to note the course the Conservative Government took in 1960 for procedural reviews. Looking favourably on a passing expression of hope by an Opposition back-bench member (Mr C. Pannell) in 1960, that there ought to be 'a small committee to keep Standing Orders on procedure under review', such a body was established for the 1962–3 Session.[1] But a senior Minister—the Leader of the House (Mr Iain Macleod)—was made a member, and he became the committee's chairman (he was, in addition, Joint Chairman of the Conservative Party). In that capacity he exercised a powerful influence and prepared each draft report. That committee considered only minor issues—and deprived observers of an interesting conflict of interests had important subjects been taken. Its impotence was not unintended.

Procedural issues in Parliament are, therefore, as political as any other. And from the references above to the Whip it would appear that the political alignment in their determination is the party alignment we find on social issues. At least, that is how the membership splits to file through the division lobbies. But what emerges in the official record is only the visible part of the iceberg of institutional politics. The rest is 'in the usual channels' or 'behind the Speaker's Chair'. If we could sound those depths our understanding of government would probably change overnight. What can be said about alignments on procedural questions, therefore, will be necessarily conjectural, and open to refutation. But that is no justification for silence.

On procedural issues the burden of the representative institution is borne, if at all, by the back-benchers on both sides, including minority groupings. Their vested interest in the reform of procedure differs from the interests of front-benchers. In their advocacy for new procedural machinery to check the administration they

1. 617 H C Deb., 5s., c. 134. And see Lord Hinchingbrooke's claim that the Select Committee on Procedure in 1959 '. . . was left leaderless because it had nobody, either inside it, or outside it, who had sufficient power to compel it to make cogent decisions on public business', *ibid*, c. 1320.

seek to extend private members' opportunities for, and in, debate. A few with a philosophical bent seek to quench their thirst for democracy in government; some wish to embarrass the Government, or to win publicity for themselves, or divert it from others; and some may see a strong and viable House of Commons as the guardian of their economic interests. But in general, in seeking reform, back-benchers seek to hold, or to redress, the Executive-Legislative balance in favour of the legislature.

The role of the government front bench is different. In all the advocacy for enhancing the power of the House of Commons, vis-à-vis the Executive, they are evasive or, at best, conciliatory. The title 'Leader' of the House is a euphemism for 'manager' of the House. His task is to manœuvre, and sometimes to bargain, with reformists, with intent to gain a position of tactical advantage. Or, in the last resort, he puts the procedural issue to a vote—with the Whip on. Above all, his goal is to retain control of the House for his government, and strive to keep adverse publicity to a minimum. Advised by an expanding Civil Service—both in power and numbers—he will yield procedural ground to back-benchers with distinct reluctance; and usually he will take more than he gives.

The Opposition front bench, on the other hand, is noticeably reticent—at most, ultra-cautious when it comes to procedural reform (which is to the advantage of back-benchers). Its members are closer to the threshold of power than anyone else on the Opposition side. They are lukewarm about change; they see themselves with political worlds to win and cannot be enthusiastic about proposals that they take new procedural chains with them. They have to placate the reformist back-bencher, possibly yield with nebulous acquiescence, or, at worst, leave him for the Government to handle.[1]

1. When newly appointed Labour 'shadow' Minister Mr Charles Pannell announced that he would use his good fortune in winning a private-member's-day ballot to discuss procedural reform on 15 March 1963, his 'reforming' motion read simply: 'That this House resolves to maintain Parliament as the paramount forum of the nation, and to bring its practices and procedures into line with the needs of 1963.' (*The Guardian*, 22, 28 February, and 11 March 1963.)

In the clamour for procedural reform in 1963 the Leader of the Opposition (Harold Wilson) said: 'I cannot see any major change that I would like to introduce.'

A study of the reform of Commons procedure, therefore, is better seen as a study of the 'ins' and 'outs' of power rather than a study of the 'ins' and 'outs' of government. There is a conflict of procedural interest in the chamber, but it is not the conflict to be seen on social issues; it is a contest of the interested back-bencher versus the rest. Something like this was implicit in W. G. Runciman's recent reminder that 'even democracies are oligarchies'. That, he says, 'requires us to assess the practical workings of democracy by rather different criteria from those envisaged by its earlier proponents.'[1] In the procedural struggle of House of Commons versus the Executive there is more in common between two front-benchers, one of whom is a member of the Government and one a member of the Opposition, than between a front-bencher and a back-bencher of the same party. The front-bench political élite groups in the House have a coincidence of interest in power; neither group is particularly anxious that the floor of the House should develop in efficiency as the national forum wherein their power—vis-à-vis the rank and file—may be challenged. Both élites are sympathetic to trends that remove uncertainty and unpredictable elements from parliamentary debate. That is, both are opposed to the development of a wider scope for open politics in the parliamentary process.[2]

He did not participate in the Pannell debate. But when the clamour continued into 1964—an election year—a new attitude was demanded. Wilson announced on the hustings, but not in the House, that his party would effect changes if elected to govern. But his commitment was non-specific. He promised less use of the Whip, and more use of the non-specialised select committees such as the Public Accounts Committee and the Estimates Committee (when the reformists wanted specialised committees). But he did not mention the ancient procedures, many of which, as confusing as they are, bolster the status and authority of the party élites over their rank and file. (*The Listener*, 21 November 1963, and the *Guardian*, 4 July 1964.)

1. W. G. Runciman, *Social Science and Political Theory* (CUP, 1963), p. 82.

2. This thesis is not new. It was forcefully made more than half a century ago by Hilaire Belloc and C. Chesterton who saw the front benches as 'one close oligarchical corporation'. *The Party System* (Swift, London, 1911). See Part II 'The Governing Group'. (This reference is due to Mr N. Blewett, University of Adelaide.) And in this respect note the cry of Conservative Cyril Osborne (Louth) from the Opposition back-benches in January 1965: 'It seems to me the usual channels have become a kind of "Butskellian in-and-out-club", a self-perpetuating oligarchy which does not consult private members of their rights.' (705 H C Deb., 5s., c. 408.)

In the context of this procedural consensus there has been a developing procedural take-over in the House of Commons. Not only have party leaders of both sides preferred party committees to parliamentary committees, but little by little in this century the House has lost ground to the government of the day and there has been only a modicum of objection, if any, from the Opposition front bench. Many of the old procedures designed to enable the representative body to check, to oppose, to delay, and to enquire, have from time to time been modified to remove particular impediments to the attainment of the Government's will. The trend is well recognised. It has been depicted in many dramatic titles— 'The Passing of Parliament', 'Bureaucracy Triumphant', 'Can Parliament Survive?', etc., etc.—but it has seldom been seen in the circumstances of representative government to be a natural political phenomenon. Take-overs of deliberative bodies whose purpose is collective decision-making are simply the processes of politics. Forces are always at work to control councils, public meetings, conferences, or groups. Parliament is no exception. Its respective Houses have always been subject to controlling forces, sometimes from within and sometimes from without—from kings, courtiers, cabals, cliques, and cabinets—with varying degrees of success. Once in control the controllers are usually anxious to minimise threats to their power; they seek to repress political activity within their field of jurisdiction for the simple purpose of making their controlling task easier—and lasting.

But when a body is the principal representative assembly in an aspiring democracy the essential question is 'what degree of control' or 'what degree of limitation on the political process' can be tolerated. In every governing circumstance there can be too much or too little restriction on discussion according to the values the observer, or the participant, holds about democratic government. But for the student of human groups the record of each controlling move is in itself an essay in politics. In the determination of the procedures of the House of Commons there is a point beyond which party back-benchers will not accept restraint upon their political activity, or at which they will be driven to bi-lateral or even multi-lateral combination against members of the front benches; there will be another point beyond which the Opposition front bench will not go in the suppression of the process of politics either as a sup-pressor or as the suppressed; and, ultimately, there is another point beyond which the electorate will not tolerate limitations upon the activity of elected members in what they see to be the people's Parliament. It cannot be emphasised too much that the process of procedural change is a political one. Consequently, it is not enough simply to assert that there is now a cabinet dictatorship in the House of Commons. Undoubtedly, due to the sanctions reinforcing party discipline, a government nowadays enjoys much more of its own way in this respect than it did in the nineteenth century, and members on the Opposition front bench have much less trouble in persuading supporters of their procedural wisdom. But the counter-vailing pressures from back-benchers with electorates to please, and with political reputations to make, ought not to be discounted.

Recently, one member, after thirty-eight years in the House, claimed: '. . . ever since I can recollect, very few honourable members have concerned themselves unduly about procedure'.[1] The truth of this can be taken in two ways. First it may illustrate the strength of party discipline and the willingness of members to leave procedural matters to the party leaders. Or, alternatively, it may acknowledge the strength and the influence of back-benchers when they have moved in the direction of procedural reform or to resist the reforms initiated by others. In this they have been far from unsuccessful. For example, the three select committees of the House having financial significance—the committees for Public Accounts, for Estimates, and for Nationalised Industries (to be examined in Chapter 4), are all monuments to back-benchers' reforming efforts. And in each case the efforts were multi-party. Back-benchers have not been without influence in their respective party rooms. When-ever they have shown signs of alignment on procedural issues with their counterparts on the other side their respective leaders have been

1. E. Shinwell (Labour), 617 HC Deb., 5s., c. 78.

all attention. Back-benchers in the House of Commons get the procedures they deserve—in a political process.

Procedure and the Constitution

The political struggle in the House of Commons over the application and the reform of the financial procedures, and the patent front-bench (particularly government-side) manœuvres when under back-bench pressure, have been blurred, and sometimes obscured, by the intrusion of constitutional terminology. The authority of the Constitution is sometimes imported in restraint of reform. It is necessary, therefore, before proceeding further, to consider the relevance of the Constitution to the House's procedures generally, and particularly to the financial procedures.

The Constitution of the United Kingdom is notoriously difficult to define. Yet it is unreal to question its authority in government. As a consequence of its obscurities the adjective 'constitutional' has many uses as an instrument of government. Indeed, in an age of reform it is a renowned weapon of conservatism. It has from time to time been appended to the major components of the House's procedure and it has enhanced their prestige and prolonged their retention. But not every student of the Constitution would agree that the methods of the House should command constitutional authority. A senior clerk of the House of Commons, for example, contends that 'The practice and the Standing Orders of the House of Commons are not contained in the constitutional documents of this country such as they are. They are mostly too domestic to be magnified to constitutional status and are too much subject to alteration and experiment to be formally confined within the relative rigidity that status would impose.'[1] But, at the other extreme, the historian and Conservative MP Sir Kenneth Pickthorn contends that 'changed bits of procedure add up to changed bits of the Constitution'.[2] More specifically, Dr K. C. Wheare points to a

1. F. G. Allen, 'Procedure in Colonial Legislatures' in *Parliamentary Affairs* (Summer 1955), vol VIII, no. 3.
2. 443 HC Deb., 5s., c. 1623.

financial Standing Order of the House (at present No. 82) giving Ministers of the Crown almost monopoly rights in initiating financial proposals as 'a major constitutional principle',[1] whereas Sir William Anson suggested that the same Order 'could be altered [as it has been] almost as easily as a College by-law, quite as easily as a rule of the Marylebone Cricket Club'.[2] There is no clear boundary line; indeed, it becomes increasingly evident in British politics that the bounds of the Constitution are where you draw them. And there is always a clash of interests in such a definition. The appellation 'constitutional' has a profound effect upon the disposition and the exercise of the power of the State.

There should be greater profit from a study that defers the issue about the parliamentary procedures being, or not being, 'constitutional' and views them in the light that Professor Laski viewed the British Constitution in general. Its 'principles and forms', he claimed, 'do not operate in a vacuum of abstract reason. They are a method intended to secure the attainment of certain ends; they are shaped to the purposes of these ends.'[3] The intention, therefore, is to arrange a juxtaposition of procedural forms and political ends in matters of financial business.

It is, however, necessary to justify the assumption that one part of the procedure of the House of Commons, the financial part, may be separated and considered in isolation from the rest. Both Bagehot and Laski warned against this approach. Bagehot would not accept that the House of Commons had any special function with regard to finance 'different from its function with respect to other legislation'. The volume of financial legislation, he asserted, 'does not indicate a diversity of nature or compel an antagonism of treatment'.[4] Laski's contention was that 'the examination and control of finance is not a separate and special function of the House of

---

1. K. C. Wheare, *The Statute of Westminster* (fifth edition, OUP, 1953), p. 13.
2. W. R. Anson, *The Law and Custom of the Constitution* (fourth edition, OUP, 1922), vol I, p. 272.
3. Harold J. Laski, *Parliamentary Government in England* (Allen and Unwin, 1938), p. 20.
4. Bagehot, *op. cit.*, p. 154.

Commons. . . . By deciding what to do in other spheres, the House
largely decides by inference what it is to do in the financial sphere.'[1]
And it was R. G. (later Sir Ralph) Hawtrey, the British Treasury's
first economist, who put this argument succinctly. He placed a high
price on words and claimed that 'financial policy is a function (in a
mathematical sense) of all other policies'.[2] These arguments are
convincing. They suggest that the quantum of expenditure, or of
revenue, is the consequence of policy decisions; they infer that if the
House looked after policy the fiscal millions would look after themselves; and they held that financial isolationism, as contemplated
here, is unreal, if not misleading. But in the House of Commons
there already exists an 'antagonism' of treatment in matters of
money. The whole corpus of the financial procedures emphasises
the sanctity of pounds, shillings, and pence; every proposal that
imposes 'a charge upon the people' or 'a charge upon the public
revenue' is liable to consideration by means of specially designed
procedures that give precedence to the cash implications. The complexity of the whole process is notorious. It commands separate
examination, in the first instance, at least. And there is possibly no
better method of unravelling its mysteries than that adopted by the
most erudite editor that Erskine May's *Parliamentary Practice* has
known. That is, the method used by the late Lord Campion.

1. Laski, *op. cit.*, p. 145.
2. R. G. Hawtrey, *The Exchequer and the Control of Expenditure* (London, 1921),
p. 28.

2

CAMPION'S FOUR RULES OF
FINANCIAL PROCEDURE

Until Sir Gilbert (later Lord) Campion (Clerk of the House of Commons 1937–48) edited a completely revised edition (the fourteenth) of Erskine May's *Parliamentary Practice*, published in 1946, the financial procedures of the House were beyond the comprehension of outside observers of Parliament, and also, it seems, many insiders. Both John Hatsell's *Precedents* (vol III 1784) and Erskine May's first edition (1844) made point of the confusion the procedures caused even in handling the relatively small budgets of governments before the extension of the franchise. In 1876 Sir Reginald Palgrave (Clerk of the House 1886–1900) asked: 'What chance has a new member of comprehending, even to a partial degree, the financial operations of his first Session?'[1] And year by year the confusion has continued. Even as recently as 1963 a professor of government in England had reason to dismiss the financial process as 'absolute gibberish'.[2] The value of Campion's contribution was that he synthesised from the diverse and confusing arrangements of the House in getting financial proposals to the statute book what he called four 'rules' of financial behaviour. These are the rules the House observes in the consideration of any proposal that comes

1. *Quarterly Review*, vol 141, p. 247. (An anonymous article usually attributed to Sir Reginald Palgrave.)

2. See Professor W. J. M. Mackenzie, 'The Plowden Report: a translation', *The Guardian*, 25 May 1963.

C

before it, should it contain either a charge upon the people (a tax) or a charge upon the public revenue (expenditure).

From the first it must be emphasised that Campion's 'rules' do not relate to the financial select committees. It will be shown (chapter 4) that these committees now operate almost independently of the legislative process. In brief, the four 'rules' are:[1]

Rule 1:   *The financial initiative of the Crown*—Any proposal for a charge [i.e. bringing an increased burden upon the Consolidated Fund, or upon the people] cannot be taken into consideration unless demanded by the Crown or recommended from the Crown.

Rule 2:   *The preliminary consideration of financial charges in a Committee of the Whole House*—A charge must first be considered in a Committee of the Whole House, and the resolution of the committee, when agreed to by the House, forms a necessary preliminary to the bill or clause by which the charge is authorised.

Rule 3:   *The legislative authorisation and appropriation of charges*—A charge does not acquire full validity until authorised by legislation; it must originate in the House of Commons and be appropriated in the same Session.

Rule 4:   *Intervals between stages of financial business*—Not more than one stage of a charging resolution or of a bill founded upon such a resolution can be taken on the same day.

Campion's contribution was to explain the financial complex globally rather than as a succession of individual processes. He has left us the only examination that makes complete sense. His 'rules' are not expressions of Standing Orders *per se*, they are simply a synthesis of innumerable precedents, Standing Orders, and statutes relating to financial business. Even though he calls them 'rules', they are expositive rather than prescriptive. Prescription is in their component parts.

Briefly, and by way of introduction to an examination of the rules, it can be said that the first acts in restraint of politics in the

1. These 'rules' remain the basis of the financial chapters of Erskine May's *Parliamentary Practice* (see seventeenth edition, 1964), p. 713.

financial-legislative process; it limits initiative on the part of private members in matters of finance. The remaining rules are designed ostensibly to encourage the clash of ideas and to stimulate the process of open compromise in the representative assembly. But in their modern application, particularly since 1832, and more particularly since the development of mass, disciplined, political parties, the restrictiveness of the first rule has been intensified, whilst the others have been substantially abridged in their intended democratic effect. Front-benchers have won power, back-benchers have lost it.

Rule 1: *The financial initiative of the Crown*

The first rule is widely known. It preserves to Ministers of the Crown a virtual monopoly of the parliamentary initiative in proposing increases in public expenditure or in taxation. This is one monopoly in the modern state that has so far escaped legal restraint. It removes a large area of legislation from the processes of open politics in the representative chamber. 'On common subjects', said Bagehot, 'any member can propose anything, but not on money—the Minister alone can propose to tax the people.'[1] And to this must be added: can propose the expenditure of public money. This, it is claimed, is 'a major constitutional principle'.[2] In its origin it is one of the oldest of the financial practices that the House observes, and nowadays, with the growth of governmental participation in national economic affairs, its parliamentary importance has multiplied a thousand-fold.

Although it finds written expression in a Standing Order of 1713, the rule is basically as old as the House of Commons itself. The Crown has always demanded finance of its Parliament, and the Commons, since winning their predominance in financial issues, have granted only in response to that demand. The Great Charter (1215), declaring that consent was a necessary precedent to taxation, and the 1306 enactment of Edward I (*Statutum de Tallagio non*

1. Bagehot, *op. cit.*, p. 154.
2. Wheare, *op. cit.*, p. 13.

Concedendo) secured for the Commons an indispensable financial function. In their performance of it, and in insisting that the King should 'live of his own' (paradoxically, had he done so their power would have been undermined), they were aware of the obloquy that taxation levies brought. They were '. . . traditionally in favour of royal economy' and 'abstained from taking the initiative in offering money to the Crown'.[1] They were reluctant even to give advice to the Crown lest it 'should lead to expense for which they might be held responsible'.[2] None of the subsequent declarations of the financial status of the Commons—the Petition of Grievance, the Petition of Right, the Bill of Rights, or the Parliament Acts—express it otherwise. 'The Crown demands, the Commons grant and the Lords assent to the grant' was Erskine May's oft-repeated, pre-1911, definition of the financial relationship.[3]

With the Crown's right of financial initiative firmly established it was not surprising that the Commons within twenty years of the Revolution Settlement (on 11 December 1706) should resolve 'That this House will receive no Petition for any sum of Money relating to public Service, but what is recommended from the Crown.'[4] And that six and a half years later—11 June 1713—they should perpetuate that resolution in the form of a Standing Order, which, with amendments, remains to this day (at present Standing Order No. 82).[5]

At the time of the adoption of the 1706 resolution the Commons were being troubled by one of the consequences of the strictness of their new 'appropriation' control. Some of the taxes granted to the Crown provided more revenue than the Commons had allocated for expenditure. But the Crown's use of the surplus was prohibited by the appropriation provisions attached to the grants. There were unspent balances, and 'Lacking any executive responsibility, the Commons could find no use of their own for this money except to apply it to the satisfaction of the claims of individuals. Petitions for pecuniary relief multiplied enormously. . . .'[6]

1. Erskine May (seventeenth edition, 1964), p. 719.
2. Anson, *op. cit.*, p. 29.   3. Erskine May (first edition, 1844), p. 324.
4. XV C.J. 211.   5. XVII C.J. 417.
6. Erskine May (seventeenth edition, 1964), p. 721.

The 1713 Order, therefore, was a written expression of a well-established practice for a new and particular end. It declared a permanent prohibition in the House on private member financial initiative arising per medium of petitions. It extended a practice that was evolved as a defence against the extravagance of the monarch to become also a defence against the extravagance of the House. And, as petitions at that time were the primary basis of non-Crown initiative, the Order of 1713 has been summarised as applying 'to private members proposals which could thus only be brought forward if the King's recommendation was given to them as of grace'.[1]

It was one thing to permit the Crown the sole right of financial initiative—and it must be understood that, as the eighteenth century progressed, that right became vested in the Crown's Ministers—but the jurisdiction of the Commons, upon the receipt of the instrument of that initiative, was entirely another matter. In keeping with the notion of parliamentary sovereignty the Commons' 'grant' of finance meant much more than mere Commons' 'assent'. It was widely claimed that representatives were free to determine the ultimate grant as they thought fit. John Hatsell in his *Precedents*, published in 1781, recorded 'That the Commons . . . took upon themselves the authority of judging as well of the nature *as of the quantum* of the particular services recommended to them by the Crown. . . .'[2] And Erskine May, writing in 1841, asserted that 'On the opening of Parliament the King directs estimates of the sums required for the various departments of the public service to be laid before the House, *but the amount of these may be varied by the commons at pleasure.*' May's qualification was simply that 'grants of money for *objects* not included in the estimates cannot be made without the King's recommendation being signified'. May also pointed out that the King, 'though he originates these grants, has no further power in matters of taxation and supply than that of giving his assent to bills which have been agreed to by both Houses

1. HC 149 (Session 1936–7), p. iv.
2. John Hatsell, *Precedents* (third edition), vol III, pp. 179–80. (Italics added.)

of Parliament'.[1] And, as for taxation, May wrote: '*The Crown has no concern in the nature and distribution of taxes*, but the foundation of all taxation is its necessity for the public service, as declared by the Crown through its constitutional advisers.'[2]

Two famous Clerks of the House of Commons, therefore, who worked closer than anyone to the procedures, and who sought to record their underlying principles, gave the rule a substantially different interpretation from that we know today. Its modern and restrictive application came with democracy. The widening bases of representation in the House brought not only new members with new values but also provoked changes in procedure that narrowed the legislative-financial freedom that elected members had hitherto claimed as theirs. The trend has continued to the point today where, as a modern Clerk of the House has explained, 'if an amendment [i.e. from a private member] might under any conceivable circumstances involve one single person in paying more tax, it is out of order'.[3]

The main limitations upon the rights of members to amend financial legislation were imposed about mid-nineteenth century. But not without confusion. Joseph Hume, for example, was incredulous in 1840 upon finding that he could not move to substitute 'a tax on the descent of real property' in lieu of the Chancellor of the Exchequer's proposal for 'customs and excise duties'. 'Does the Chancellor mean to say', Hume asked, 'that no man can propose a new tax in this Committee but the Chancellor of the Exchequer?'[4] Hume lost. Yet, as late as 1851, Mr Speaker Shaw-Lefevre ruled that '. . . if the honourable member meant to impose increased taxation . . . it was not necessary that he should have the recommendation of the Crown'.[5] It is pertinent too that May's assertion that 'The Crown has no concern in the nature and distribution of

1. T. E. May, 'The Imperial Parliament' in *Knights Store of Knowledge* (London, 1841), p. 102. (Italics added.) And see *Penny Cyclopaedia* (London, 1840), vol XVII, p. 271.

2. Erskine May (first edition, 1844), p. 324. (Italics added.)

3. Sir Edward Fellowes, HC 110 (1957), Q. 240.

4. *Mirror of Parliament*, vol IV, pp. 3040–62.

5. CXV HC Deb., 3s., c. 660.

taxes' remained in his *Parliamentary Practice* until 1893, when, after his death, it was omitted, without comment, from the tenth edition.

To impose the new restrictions on members in this respect, two changes in the Standing Order of 1713 were necessary. The first was adopted by the House on 25 June 1852, in the final days of Lord Derby's minority government (with Mr Disraeli as Chancellor of the Exchequer), when 'the fear of social revolution was present in the mind of British aristocrats' and when Derby was insistent that political power 'should not be thrown into the hands of mere numbers at the expense of property and intelligence'.[1] It was also a time when the Government was on tenterhooks lest a back-bencher should embarrass it with a motion to initiate new tariff duties. A Sessional and Standing Orders Revision Committee, comprising, amongst others, procedural purists such as W. E. Gladstone, Evelyn Denison, and Wilson Patten, without explanation, listed the 1713 Standing Order as one of the 'cautionary' procedures relating to public business. Then, upon consideration of that committee's report, the House, without recorded debate, 'replaced' the 1713 Order with one which read:

That this House will receive no Petition for any Sum of Money, relating to public Service, *or proceed upon any Motion for granting any Money* but what is recommended from the Crown.[2]

This unqualified extension of the Standing Order to include 'any motion . . .' had, of course, profound parliamentary implications. And undoubtedly the modern significance of the rule dates not, as is often claimed, from the time of Queen Anne,[3] but from that amendment.

It is also significant that the Parliament was dissolved within a week of the 1852 amendment, and that Derby went to the electorate with a policy claiming that 'more important than the revision of the tariff laws' was 'the preservation of British institutions against the

1. W. D. Jones, *Lord Derby and Victorian Conservatism* (Blackwell, 1956), pp. 163–7.
2. CVII CJ 353. (New words italicised.)
3. For example Sir E. Barker, *Britain and the British People* (OUP, 1955), p. 30; Sir Ivor Jennings, *Parliament* (CUP, 1948), p. 250.

rising tide of democracy'.[1] Derby also boasted of his government's efforts 'to supply some barrier against the current of that continually increasing and encroaching democratic influence . . . which is bent on throwing the whole power and authority of the government nominally into the hands of the masses, but practically and really into those of demagogues and republicans'.[2]

Surprisingly, the Derby-Disraeli change proved to be inadequate in keeping the Treasury immune from the pressures of representatives. Members found simple means for evasion. They would add a qualification to any bill they wished to introduce, or any amendment they wished to move, if it sought to increase expenditure, to the effect that the charge involved would be met 'out of monies to be provided by Parliament'. Then they would hold, not without success, that the limitations of the Standing Order of 1713 (as amended in 1852) did not apply immediately, but only later, when the House ultimately came to provide the money (i.e. when the relevant Estimate was introduced). And then, at that later stage, if the charge was objected to, members would urge in reply 'that the faith and credit of the country had been pledged to the outlay'.

It was to the above loophole that C. J. Ayrton (MP for Tower Hamlets) directed his attention in 1866, and achieved the second change to the 1713 Standing Order. Ayrton was a back-bench supporter of (and later an embarrassment to) Mr Gladstone, and he was soon to become a Minister. Ayrton moved for change, without select committee preliminaries, one week after Gladstone's ill-fated Reform Bill had been introduced, and after the House had endured several weeks of confusion over financial amendments relating to compensation provisions for farmers in the Cattle Diseases Protection Bill. It is significant that Speaker Evelyn Denison, noted defender of members' rights, was absent owing to illness, and that Ayrton admitted his proposal 'was not entirely his own'. Gladstone was prompt in thanking Ayrton and in giving the proposal his full

1. W. D. Jones, *op. cit.*, pp. 163–7.
2. cxix HC Deb., 3s., c. 1013. Quoted by F. E. Gillespie, *Labour and Politics in England 1850–1867* (Duke, 1927), p. 99.

support. Ayrton's motion was carried (20 March 1866) and the Standing Order was amended to read, as it reads today (Standing Order No. 82):

That this House will receive no Petition for any sum relating to Public Service, or proceed upon any Motion for a grant or charge upon Public Revenue, *whether payable out of the Consolidated Fund or out of monies to be provided by the Parliament*, unless recommended from the Crown. (New words italicised.)[1]

About the time of the 1866 amendment the rule of the financial initiative of the Crown found favour with both J. S. Mill and Walter Bagehot. The former claimed that 'moderation' in public expenditure, and 'care and judgment in the detail of its application', can only be expected when the 'executive government . . . is made responsible for the plans and calculations on which disbursements are grounded'.[2] Bagehot held that the Executive must hold 'sole financial charge'. '. . . all policy', he said, 'depends on money, and it is in adjusting the relative goodness of action and policies that the executive is employed.'[3] Both men were fearful of democratic representation. Their common view, wrote R. H. S. Crossman recently, was that the great issue of the 1860's was 'how to prevent the party politician, for purely opportunist reasons, making concessions to democracy which would substitute government by ignorant and brute numbers for government by discussion'.[4] And even when Sir William Anson reviewed the rule in 1886 he saw it as '. . . the great safeguard of the tax-payer against the casual benevolence of the House wrought upon by the eloquence of a private member; against a scramble for public money among unscrupulous politicians bidding against one another for the favour of a democracy'.[5]

1. For Ayrton's explanation of the procedural problem, see CLXXXII HC Deb. 3s., cc. 591–603. *And see* 121 CJ 182.
2. *Representative Government* (Blackwell edition, 1946), p. 163.
3. Bagehot, *op. cit.*, p. 155.
4. Introduction to Walter Bagehot, *The English Constitution, op. cit.*, p. 7.
5. Anson, *op. cit.*, p. 272.

Undoubtedly the Standing Order of 1713 (as amended) has been embraced, particularly by modern governments, as the expression of the procedural means for keeping parliamentary representatives at bay in the name of economic stability. Governments have sought successfully to gain an increasingly restrictive interpretation of it, and it now has political significance of the highest order. When we praise the 'Westminster Model' for providing strong government we, in effect, acknowledge the power that this rule gives the Executive over the representative body. Although it is claimed to be 'a major constitutional principle' it is strange that it has not yet found its historian. British Constitutional writers have repeated superficial comments about it. Perhaps its modern political significance is illustrated by its universal prescription, albeit variously expressed, wherever the British-type system of government has been established overseas. Lord Durham, for example, was critical of the failure to observe its basic principle in Canada in 1839. He asserted that '. . . as long as any member of the Assembly may, without restriction, propose a vote of public money, so long will the Assembly retain in its hands the powers which it everywhere abuses, of misapplying that money'. Such a system, he claimed, gave 'undue influence to particular individuals or parties'.[1] Durham had the rule given its first legal expression in the British North America Act 1840 (the Act of Union). This was a comprehensive and restrictive declaration which, no doubt, had an influence upon subsequent developments in Westminster. It forbade the introduction of any proposal (whether by bill or by amendment) to increase expenditure or to increase taxation which did not first have the recommendation of the Governor.[2] But, ultimately, when the rule was re-expressed in the British North America Act 1867, it was liberalised to the extent of merely declaring it to be unlawful to 'adopt or pass' proposed increases to expenditure or taxation without the recommendation of the Governor-General.[3]

When the rule was written into the Australian Constitution at the

---

1. R. Coupland (ed.), *The Durham Report* (abridged, OUP, 1945), p. 148.
2. 3 & 4 Vict., c. 35, LVII.   3. 30 Vict., c. 3, 54s.

end of the nineteenth century the architects, mostly practising politicians from the several colonial Parliaments, were suspicious of Executive strength in the new federal body. They liberalised the rule even further. In line with the Westminster Standing Order (as distinct from Westminster practice of the day), they omitted reference to taxation, so as to leave scope for private members to introduce proposals on the tariff. And, accordingly, Section 56 of the Constitution provided simply that expenditure proposals 'shall not pass' without a recommendation from the Governor-General. It is interesting that in subsequent years, both in Canada and Australia, the respective Houses, under the influence of powerful Executives, have adopted all the restrictive interpretations of the rule—and more—that have been made at Westminster.

Successive governments at Westminster have shown their sensitivity to the fact that this rule has no firmer base than a Standing Order of the House of Commons. It has been jealously guarded from any amendment that would favour the power of private members. A select committee appointed in 1937, specifically to enquire into the rule's restrictive effects, was limited in its terms of reference 'to the unimpaired maintenance of the principles [it] embodied . . .'.[1] And before a recent Select Committee on Procedure the Financial Secretary to the Treasury (Rt Hon Henry Brooke) emphasised:

> . . . that the maintenance of the principle is considered more important now with the enormous growth of the sums paid out of the Exchequer under modern legislation when the Government's activities extend so widely into social and industrial fields . . .[2]

In testing support for the retention of the rule, and its present interpretation, it should be acknowledged that its basic principle existed long before Cabinet government emerged, and that its post-1850 restrictive application was the product of political conditions preceding the development of nationally based political parties.

1. HC 149 (Session 1936–7), p. iii.
2. HC 110 (Session 1956–7), p. 19.

But now that governments are backed by disciplined party supporters, Anson's fears of 'unscrupulous politicians bidding against one another for the favour of a democracy' are somewhat exaggerated. Perhaps advocates of the rule would claim that in Anson's statement 'politicians' is now synonymous with 'parties' and, without the rule, unscrupulous 'parties' would now bid against one another . . . etc. But whether we like it or not party bargaining, with or without scruples, is the essence of modern democracy. It must be asked, then, why any restriction should be placed upon the free expression of party conflict through formal motions in legislative debate—whatever their financial effect? The rule, in its modern application, manifests a distrust of the political process in Parliament, and also a distrust of politicians, parties, and pressure groups. And this, in effect, is a distrust of democracy.

Furthermore, Brooke's justification, based on the sheer magnitude of public expenditure today, is a *non sequitur*. The increasing size and the increasing political importance of expenditure plans makes more desirable their free discussion, and the expression of the opinion of the House, on alternative proposals 'that extend so widely into social and industrial fields'. But the rule, obviously, is designed to act in restraint of such activity.

Governments embrace the restrictive interpretation of this rule because it suppresses politics in Parliament and makes their task easier. It protects parties in government from the political embarrassment of having to vote against a wide range of alternative proposals, initiated in other parts of the House, and designed to appeal to the electorate. It keeps back-bench dissidents in their place on legislative-financial issues which is a restraint front-benchers on both sides support. And it helps to suppress the financial initiative that could, in some circumstances, facilitate the birth of new parties. Moreover, it provides governments, in the name of a traditional procedure, claimed to be 'as old as the reign of Queen Anne', with a powerful controlling technique 'ready', influential', and 'easy to get obeyed'.

But it must be admitted that the rule expresses a well-tried procedure, and that it gains increasing popularity midst modern demands for strong government. President De Gaulle, for example, by having it expressed in the Constitution of the Fifth Republic, made it a basic part of his plan for the subordination of the French National Assembly.[1] And the rule was of substantial assistance to President Kwame Nkrumah in his successful quest to subordinate the formal Opposition in the Ghanaian National Assembly.[2] It finds its expression wherever the British model is established overseas. We should be mindful, therefore, that when the Westminster model is acclaimed for providing the machinery of formal Opposition it ought to be acknowledged that this rule provides an important means by which that Opposition is successfully restrained.

Rule 2: *The preliminary consideration of financial charges in a Committee of the Whole House*

This second rule is designed to act in the interests of politics. But whether it continues to have that effect is open to question. Of seventeenth-century origin, it expresses the House's choice of a particular 'preliminary' procedure for its financial business. By excluding its Speaker, and by appointing a chairman in his stead, the House came to function as a committee of all its members and thereby enjoyed less formal methods of deliberation at the initial stage of every financial proposal. As early seventeenth-century Speakers were royal nominees, the procedure is usually associated with the House's anxiety to be rid of the King's influence during financial discussions. But, in spite of its plausibility, some historians of that period have lacked enthusiasm for this interpretation. Professor Wallace Notestein, for example, posed the question 'was the practice designed to get rid of the Speaker' and he concluded that 'it is impossible to say'. He would claim no more than the procedure appeared 'rather accidentally', 'excited little comment', and that 'the Commons found it a convenience of the Committee

1. Albert Mavrinac, *Organization and Procedure of the National Assembly of the Fifth French Republic* (Hansard Society), p. 7; and see W. Pickles, 'Special Powers in France —Article 16 in Practice', *Public Law* (Spring, 1963).
2. S. A. R. Bennion, *The Constitutional Laws of Ghana* (Butterworth, 1962), p. 38.

plan that the Speaker could no longer regulate their debates. . . .'[1]
And there is similar scepticism in Professor Neale's findings that the
Commons in an 'unpremeditated way . . . stumbled upon the
substance of a new procedural device, the Committee of the Whole
House . . .'.[2] But one thing is clear. In its origin the Committee of
the Whole House offered members a wider and more satisfying
freedom in parliamentary deliberation.

As early as 1628, John Eliot, upon whom restraints on politics
were later to become so painful, saw the Committee of the Whole
House as '. . . the way that led most to the truth. It was the more
open way. It admitted of every man's adding his reasons, and making answer upon hearing the reason and arguments of other men'.[3]
And he claimed 'by answer and reply the discussion might be free in
the counterchange of reason and opinion. The latter is not admittable
in the House, where, to avoid contestation and disorder, which re-
plies and contradictions might introduce, and to preserve the gravity,
no man may speak in one day and to one business above once, though
he would change opinion, which in Committee is allowable.'[4]

And Henry Scobell (Clerk of the House of Commons 1649–59)
recorded that the House used the Committee of the whole for
'. . . bills of great concernment . . . Bills to impose a tax, or raise
money from the people'. The procedure in his opinion provided
for 'fuller debates' for 'members have liberty to speak as often as
they shall see cause, to one Question . . .'.[5]

In its origin, therefore, the procedure provided advantages in
debate. It was later in the seventeenth century that the House
adopted a nomenclature to distinguish the financial purposes pursued in the committee. As Lord Campion pointed out, a clear division of functions became evident during the reign of Charles II.

1. Wallace Notestein, *The Winning of the Initiative by the House of Commons* (The
Raleigh Lecture in History, 1924), p. 33.
2. J. E. Neale, *The Elizabethan House of Commons* (Jonathan Cape, 1949), p. 378.
3. John Forster, *Sir John Eliot. A Biography 1592–1632* (Longmans, Green, 1864),
vol II, p. 188.
4. *ibid*, vol II, p. 263.
5. Henry Scobell, *Memorials of the Method and Manner of Proceedings in Parliament in
Passing Bills* (London, 1689), p. 49.

'The Committee of Supply raised money by the imposition of recognised taxes, long part of the fiscal system (which were so assessed to bring in roughly the same amount on each occasion) whereas the Committee of Ways and Means came into existence for the purpose of devising new ways of raising money.'[1] Both committees were recognised as having a separate identity and enjoyed a continuity of existence throughout each session. Both dealt with taxation.

It was in the next century, after Pitt's plans for one Consolidated Fund matured into legislation in 1787, that the present-day functions of the two committees became established. The Committee of Supply voted grants for the annual expenditure of the Government out of the fund, and the Committee of Ways and Means levied the taxation to bring revenue in—but in both cases the grants and the taxes were always embodied in legislation.

There also developed in the eighteenth century, but more clearly in the nineteenth as the functions of government expanded, the procedure for the preliminary consideration in a Committee of the Whole House called a 'money' committee of the financial provisions of policy bills. Such committees continue to be established today, always *ad hoc*, and are a clear application of this rule.

But it was as early as 1667 that the House made its first formal declaration of this rule. Facing the perennial problems of government by discussion, it acted on the recommendation of a select committee that had considered 'what does obstruct the proceedings of the Public Business of the House', and resolved:

. . . that if any motion be made in the House for any public aid or charge upon the People, the consideration and debate thereof ought not presently to be entered upon; but adjourned till such further day, as the House shall think fit to appoint; and then it ought to be referred to the Committee of the whole House; and their opinions to be reported thereon; before any resolution or vote of the House do pass therein.[2]

This expressed the House's post-Restoration caution in matters of finance. The Commons were not anxious to be 'rushed into ex-

1. Campion, *op. cit.*, pp. 33-4.   2. IX, C.J. 52.

penditure by the parliamentary friends of Charles 11'.[1] They were
in an ill humour for '. . . the supplies granted in the Session of 1666
had been squandered away' so they declared formally their procedure for the scrutiny of the Crown's financial needs.[2]

But when the procedure was expressed in the form of a Standing
Order on 29 March 1707 it was shortened and the permissive
'ought' of the 1667 resolution became the mandatory 'will not'.
The Standing Order read:

That this House will not proceed upon any Petition, Motion or Bill, for
granting any Money, or for releasing, or compounding, any Sum of Money
owing to the Crown, but in a Committee of the whole House.[3]

This declaration arose from conditions similar to those that
provoked the resolution of 11 December 1706 (Rule 1); it was
designed to control the consideration of frequent petitions seeking
the 'compounding' of debts due to the Crown. It was retained
during the eighteenth century, and, as Hatsell emphasised, 'very
strictly adhered to'.[4] And like the Standing Order expression of the
first rule it did not come into serious question again until 1852 and
1866.

In 1852 the Sessional and Standing Orders Revision Committee
declared this procedure to be another of those 'cautionary' methods
that the House had long followed. And it is significant that in res-
ponding to the committee's report, and as a protection 'against the
rising tide of democracy', the House (or the Derby Government),
rather than adapt the Standing Order of 1707 to the new conditions,
chose to rehabilitate the more comprehensive expression of the 1667
resolution. 'Shall' was substituted for 'ought' and the long resolution
was given Standing Order authority.[5] Presumably, the 1667 expression, in prescribing time-intervals between the preliminary

1. E. H. Davenport, *Parliament and the Taxpayer* (Skeffington, 1918), p. 119.
2. Catherine Strateman (ed.), *The Liverpool Tractate* (Columbia University Press,
1937), p. 59; and see H C 279 (Session 1857), pp. 94–5.
3. This is the earliest of the Standing Orders of the House of Commons, x v, C.J.,
367.
4. Hatsell, *op. cit.*, vol III, p. 177.   5. C V I I C.J., 353.

stages of every financial proposal, added a safeguard against hasty and ill-considered decisions being forced at the hands of mere numbers. As Erskine May put it in 1854, it helped the House... 'to guard against surprises on the part of its own Members'.[1]

Then finally, in 1866, the House, on the initiative of back-bench member C. J. Ayrton, with motives as explained above, altered the Standing Order of 1852 to read (as it still reads today, as Standing Order No. 83):

That if any motion be made in the House for any aid grant, or charge upon the Public Revenue, *whether payable out of the Consolidated Fund or out of money to be provided by Parliament,* or for any charge upon the People, the consideration and debate thereof shall not be presently entered upon, but shall be adjourned till such further day as the House shall think fit to appoint, and then it shall be referred to a Committee of the whole House before any Resolution or Vote of the House do pass therein.[2]

This second financial rule has met more than a fair share of criticism by advocates of parliamentary reform. The fact that it perpetuates the notion of a committee of the complete membership of the House encourages objection. If the best committee is a committee of one—then a committee of 630 members undoubtedly magnifies deliberative deficiencies. Bagehot ridiculed it as 'One of the most helpless exhibitions of helpless ingenuity and wasted mind . . .'.[3] And to a critic of the 1880's it was 'a crucible of confusion'.[4] Sir Courtenay Ilbert, early this century, stressed the confusion the procedure causes to continental observers. They find, he said, 'difficulty in reconciling the sense in which we use the word "Committee" when we talk of a Committee of the Whole House, with the meaning which they attach to such an expression as *commission* or *ausschuss* which means a small body appointed by a larger body'.[5] Yet in all its procedural aspects the Committee of the

1. HC 212 (Session 1854), Evidence, Q. 213.
2. 121 C.J. 182. (Words added in 1866 in italics.)
3. Bagehot, *op. cit.*, p. 136.
4. E. R. Wodehouse, *Reform of Procedure in the House of Commons* (Bath, 1881), p. 14.
5. HC 181 (Session 1906), Q. 280.

D

Whole House is a committee. It lives under terms of reference granted by the House; it has no authority other than that the House gives it; even its sittings are limited by order of the House; it is presided over by a chairman; the Speaker pleads ignorance of its proceedings; and it is obliged to report back to the House.

Criticism about the continued use of the Committee of the Whole House for financial business has been forthcoming even from the House's own Select Committees on Procedure. One reported in 1918 that it 'has the name but none of the methods of a committee . . .';[1] another asserted in 1932 that the Committee of Supply was '. . . ill equipped for enquiry', and a '. . . very imperfect instrument for the control of expenditure . . .'.[2] As recently as 1959 and 1963 'the rule that charges may not be imposed save in a committee' has been attacked by select committees as being based on 'the traditional view of the Speaker as a partisan of the Crown . . . which has long ceased to have any basis in fact' and which 'has led to much confusion and complication'.[3]

Surprisingly, it is the latter type of assertion that itself causes 'much confusion and complication'. It is a repetition of Sir Ivor Jennings' allegations of procedural anachronism. 'When kings had power,' wrote Jennings, 'and men who opposed them were likely to be cast into uttermost darkness, there was some importance in moving the Speaker, the King's representative, out of the Chair, and discussing in private whether the King should have money. . . .'[4] On the basis of that reasoning the Clerk Assistant of the House claimed in 1965 that the procedure 'could now be abandoned . . . without constitutional impropriety . . .'.[5] But the Speaker ceased to be the King's nominee, or even his 'representative', at the end of the seventeenth century. So the critics are suggesting that the rule has been redundant for well over 250 years. They imply that in all that time the procedure has been observed as an empty ritual. Is that really the case?

1. HC 121 (Session 1918), p. 115.   2. HC 129 (Session 1931–2), p. xii.
3. HC 92 (Session 1958–9), p. x; and HC 271 (Session 1962–3), pp. 8–9.
4. Jennings, *op. cit.*, p. 261
5. Mr D. W. S. Lidderdale, HC 303 (Session 1965–6), p. 6.

A better understanding of the rule (and the procedure) is to be gained by looking at it in terms of effect, rather than its origin. It will be seen that it has not been preserved on romantic notions alone.

The rule, and its application through the several financial Committees of the Whole House, in spite of its critics, still has profound parliamentary importance. It is during the stage of the preliminary consideration of a financial charge in such a committee that two worlds—that of officials and that of elected representatives—meet. It is here, and only here, that a Minister of the Crown, backed by official advice, may exercise his monopoly rights over financial initiative (our first rule). And it is here, and only here, that the representatives consider that initiative, *per se*. The resolution that emerges from the financial committee, when adopted by the House, becomes the House's own financial criterion for the subsequent legislative process. There are three important implications in this.

First, in all the subsequent stages for enshrining a financial charge in legislation, all members—front-benchers and back-benchers alike—are, theoretically, equal. As Erskine May puts it, 'Ministers are . . . in respect of the financial initiative no more privileged than private members except that, as advisers of the Crown, they are in a position to procure the communications which initiate the proceedings'.[1] If during one of the subsequent legislative stages any elected representative—Minister or private member—wishes to exercise a new financial initiative by way of an amendment proposal, to increase the tax or the expenditure charge beyond the limits of the original financial resolution, the rule requires that he must return to the financial committee and initiate a further resolution. The rule, therefore, acting in the interests of politics, provides a cautionary or 'red flag' procedure by which opportunity for specific and additional consideration must be given to all new financial charges.

But, secondly, and more importantly, with the help of Rule 1,

1. Erskine May (seventeenth edition, 1964), p. 729.

Ministers of the Crown have been able to usurp the advantages in debate that this rule affords. They have found distinct political advantages in using the resolutions of the financial Committees of the Whole House as financial criteria for the legislative process. In this way the Executive's financial initiative in a financial committee —that is, the motions based on Estimates of Expenditure in the Committee of Supply, the taxation motions in the Committee of Ways and Means, and the motions for money resolutions in the money committees—have in each case become instruments of control over the political process in the legislature. If the Executive drafts such motions in minute particularity, then the financial resolutions based upon them, when adopted by the committee, and then by the House, are similarly detailed, and, as a result, the scope for the acceptance of amendment proposals during the subsequent legislative stages can be strictly controlled, or even virtually eliminated. With this potential the procedure has given rise to voluminous and detailed Estimates of Expenditure, prolix taxation motions, and legalistic money resolutions. The control over debate exercised in this way, and the limitation thereby imposed on the freedom of members to initiate amendments to legislation, have become so consistently comprehensive in their proscriptive effect that the procedure has come to appear an unnecessary ritual, and its political purpose has been lost to the casual observer.

A third reason for the retention of a Committee of the Whole House for consideration of financial proposals, in preference to the development of a procedure based on small committees, is the simple and important fact that both the Whip and party discipline are more easily applied in divisions held in the House rather than those in the 'upstairs' committee rooms. This procedure (and the rule) finds many abolitionists, but their claims are characterised by an absence of constructive alternatives.

Rule 3: *The legislative authorisation and appropriation of charges*
This could be called the 'Rule of Law' in finance. In the interests of politics it provides that every charge upon the public revenue, and

upon the people, must pass through the legislative process, be open to scrutiny by the elected representatives, and be enacted in law. In other words it is the procedural prescription of representative consent to taxation.

As a rule of procedure this is based upon the provisions of the Bill of Rights 'That levying money for the use of the Crown by pretence of prerogative without the grant of Parliament for longer time or in other manner than the same is or shall be granted is illegal.' It is the fulcrum of the Commons' financial power; it is the statutory expression of its ultimate sanction—the power to bring any government to its knees by depriving it of finance. The rule expresses three distinct precepts of action.

First, it provides that a charge does not acquire full validity until it is authorised by legislation. This finds its origin deep in parliamentary history. In its beginning the Parliament in Britain was virtually an instrument of the King's Executive authority, it was part of the monarch's bureaucracy. But the recurring need of the Crown for 'extraordinary supply', which usually meant increased taxation, weakened the Royal hierarchy and helped to make the local communities, through their representatives, '. . . a more normal ingredient of Parliament and offered scope for the enlargement of their participation. . . .' Whereas the Commons attended only one in about every eight parliaments down to 1289, and one in three after 1290, they were missing from only four of the twenty-five assemblies between 1327 and 1336. Representatives' consent to taxation was, at this early stage of English history, seen as a wise precaution for stable government.[1] But by what means was that consent given?

It was not until late in the fourteenth century that the procedure for granting 'aids' to the Crown by 'bill' replaced the simple vote of both Houses. Stubbs claimed that 'from the end of the reign of Richard II [1400] all grants were made in the Commons with the advice and assent of the Lords in a documentary form which may be termed an Act of Parliament'. But he pointed out 'that we have very seldom any details of debate upon them or of the exact steps

1. Edward Miller, *The Origins of Parliament* (Routledge, 1960), pp. 15–20.

of the process by which they became law'.[1] Whether the bills were accorded the three readings technique of consideration is not clear. 'It is not until 1492 that the Rolls of Parliament mention more than a single reading.'[2] Yet the earliest of the Journals of the Parliament (1509) imply that the three readings procedure had long been established. 'The practice of thrice reading the bills appears however in the Journals of the two Houses so early, and from the very first Parliament of Henry VIII regarded so clearly as the established rule, that it must have full credit for antiquity; it was a matter of course.'[3]

For more than five centuries, therefore, Parliament has authorised its money grants by legislation. And the records of its struggles to apply this rule comprehensively have provided much of British parliamentary history. So the relationship of the precept to the financial process is clear—it provides that every charge (upon the public revenue or upon the people) must pass through a multi-staged procedure in both Houses of Parliament before becoming enacted law. And when we consider the procedures demanded by the second and the third of Campion's financial rules acting collectively it is obvious that the financial process, in the House of Commons alone, is long and technically involved. The two rules afford representatives with a long sequence of occasions in which to engage in a political process. But for a government wishing to expedite the job of governing, both rules, obviously, invoke seeming impediments to rapid achievement. The following chapters will explain how the rules have been retained while, at the same time, the impediments have been largely removed.

The second precept of the third rule insists that a charge, and the legislation that embodies it, must originate in the House of Commons. The Commons have always asserted that the grant of finance to the Crown is their grant, and that the role of the House of Lords in its enactment is either concurrence or rejection. An explanation of their original financial ascendancy has been made:

1. W. Stubbs, *Constitutional History of England* (Library edition, 1880), vol III, p. 496.

2. Campion, *op. cit.*, p. 22.   3. Stubbs, *op. cit.*, p. 497.

The Commons, clerk and lay, have superiority because they are representatives, unlike the magnates, they do not come to the parliament *per se* but for their communities (prepared to act in all things as if those who chose them were present in person) . . . the main business for which their consent is required, the business which cannot be carried through without them, is consent to taxation granted the King. The ultimate ascendancy of the Commons is obviously bound up with the control of Supply.[1]

It was as early as 1407 that the Commons made an issue of their claim for financial pre-eminence. Henry IV had not accorded them their accustomed privilege of first discussing his money requirements with them. The Commons remonstrated and had their superiority formally acknowledged by the King—'that grants of Supply must take their rise in the Commons, and that the resulting grants, after the Lords has assented to them, ought to be reported by the mouth of the Speaker of the House of Commons.'[2]

And five and a half centuries later the Commons still claim the same status.[3] But the Lords did not acquiesce readily in a subordinate position; many attempts were made to discard the yoke of Commons privilege, and until 1911 their position was always fortified politically by the knowledge that the necessity for their consent to financial legislation was, in fact, a power of veto in their hands. The well-known inter-House conflicts over financial matters in the troubled seventeenth century provoked some significant statements. For example, in 1671 the Lords argued their right to amend, as well as reject, financial bills—'. . . if the Lords who have the power of treating, advising, giving counsel and applying remedies, cannot amend, abate, or refuse a bill in part, by what consequence of reason can they enjoy a liberty to reject the whole?' The Commons attitude, on the other hand, was 'Your Lordships . . . have a negative to the whole.' Then, by analogy, they claimed

1. M. V. Clarke, *Mediaeval Representation and Consent* (Longmans, Green, 1936), p. 14

2. Stubbs, *op. cit.*, vol III, p. 62 *seq.* Cf. Anson *op. cit.*, p. 280.

3. As recently as April 1963 the House of Lords yielded to objections voiced against its consideration, before the House of Commons, of a proposed financial charge in the Legal Aid Bill. The Government moved the bill's withdrawal after its second reading. See 248 HL Deb., 5s., cc. 663–71, 801–8.

'The King must deny the whole of every bill, or pass it; yet this takes not away his negative voice.'[1]

In 1678 the Commons resolved to express their financial aspiration with relative finality:

> That all Aids and Supplies and Aids to His Majesty in Parliament, are the sole gift of the Commons; and all Bills for the granting of any such Aids and Supplies ought to begin with the Commons; and that it is the undoubted and sole right of the Commons to direct, limit, and appoint in such Bills, the ends, purposes, considerations and conditions, limitations and qualifications of such grants, which ought not to be changed or altered by the House of Lords.[2]

Between 1708 and 1854 the Lords caused eighteen financial bills to be postponed or rejected; and even their clash with the Commons in 1860, when they rejected Gladstone's Paper Duty Repeal Bill, left their veto intact. The financial veto was a powerful political instrument at the disposal of the hereditary body. It was only the extension of the franchise that finally made it an anachronism. The ill-judged Lord's rejection of the Finance Bill in 1909 hastened their fiscal demise. It led not only to new resolutions reasserting Commons' financial privileges, but also to a relatively conclusive declaration of them (for a specific category of business) in statute law. The Parliament Act 1911 declared in favour of the elected House and thereby gave the Commons a financial authority that its own resolutions of privilege had not attained.

The third and final precept of Rule 3—that a charge must be appropriated in the same session—refers to expenditure grants. And it too finds its origin early in the life of the House. Devised in order to prevent the Crown from spending money on objects which the Parliament had not approved, appropriation control nowadays expresses a parliamentary aspiration rather than a parliamentary attainment. Early examples of its application are to be found in the reign of Edward III (1312–77) but it was not until the Crown became almost wholly dependent upon Parliament for its revenue

1. J. Hatsell, *Precedents* (new edition, 1818), vols III–IV, pp. 405 and 423.
2. IX, C.J., 509.

that the procedure could become comprehensive in both its intention and effect.[1] In the latter part of the seventeenth century it was recognised that the hard-won financial authority of the Commons 'would be nugatory if the proceeds, even of legal taxes, could be expended at the will of the sovereign'.[2] And after the Restoration there were renewed attempts at detailed appropriation control, but it is claimed 'the Commons had not learned the value of constant control . . . their liberality to Charles, and afterwards to James II, enabled the monarchs to violate the public liberty'.[3]

Not until the latter part of the eighteenth century could it be recorded that the appropriation control was becoming comprehensive. One parliamentary observer at that time was sanguine about its effect. 'Appropriation clauses', he wrote, 'in the beginning of King William's reign . . . were very loose and general; but they continued to become more and more exact, till at last they have been brought to the utmost possible nicety, without any bad consequence, either to Prerogative or Liberty; and what is more, they seem equally agreeable to His Majesty's ministers, and the rest of his subjects and most happily adapted for the ease and security of all sides.'[4]

There is no doubt that the vital advance came in 1787 when Adam Smith in the *Wealth of Nations* proposed one Consolidated Fund. This found favour with Pitt and Parliament. A fund was created, by law, 'into which shall flow every stream of public revenue, and from whence shall issue the supply of every public service'.[5] This broke the disorder caused by assigning particular taxes to special purposes and it provided the means of infinite expenditure control through comprehensive appropriation schedules.

1. For concise reviews of early instances of appropriation control and audit see Basil Chubb, *The Control of Public Expenditure* (OUP, 1952), pp. 6–23; Paul Einzig, *The Control of the Purse* (Secker and Warburg, 1959), pp. 77–85; and Davenport, *op. cit.*, pp. 36–53.

2. A. J. V. Durell, *The Principles and Practice of the System of Control over Parliamentary Grants* (Hogg, 1917), p. 3.

3. T. Erskine May, *Constitutional History of England* (seventeenth edition, Longmans, Green, 1882), p. 99.

4. Strateman, *op. cit.*, p. 170.   5. 27 Geo III, c. 13, S. 47.

It opened the way for the financial reforms of the nineteenth century.

It was not until the 1860's, however, that Gladstone could claim that the 'circle' of parliamentary control was complete. At that stage it was evident that parliamentary appropriation was basic to the whole control system. Gladstone's expenditure circle started with the Executive's presentation to the House of Commons of annual and comprehensive estimates; it ran through the long and tedious procedures for parliamentary vote and legal appropriation, the departmental spending processes, and the keeping of annual cash accounts; the next point was the audit of accounts, on behalf of Parliament, by the Comptroller and Auditor-General, to ensure that money had been spent in accordance with the appropriations made; and finally, the circle returned to Parlaiment via the House's Committee of Public Accounts and its follow-up enquiry into the criticisms made in the auditors' report. Gladstone's circle metaphor, even a century later, still explains the formalities of the control system, but as a definition of realities it is now sadly deficient.

Public expenditure in Gladstone's day totalled about £70 millions per year. It now runs in excess of £7,000 millions (it is expected to reach £8,000 millions by 1968) and its sheer magnitude and complexity changes the whole picture. There are still annual Estimates of Expenditure, appropriations by law, a Comptroller and Auditor-General, and a Committee of Public Accounts—but their respective functions and their relative importance have altered. There is now (since 1912) an Estimates Committee to fit into the control picture, and, more importantly, the arrangements for the vast nationalised industries—the largest employers in the country— have, by and large, been deliberately placed beyond the circle's compass. But in spite of these vast changes, the appropriation precept holds—it is still part of the third rule of financial procedure.

Rule 4: *Intervals between stages of financial business*
Campion's fourth rule is as old as any of the others. Most delibera- tive bodies, as a precaution against unexpected influence, insist that

notice must be given of all subjects proposed for their consideration. But in its procedures for financial business the House of Commons has gone further. It has preserved a rule that provides that 'Not more than one stage of a charging resolution or of a bill founded upon such a resolution can be taken on the same day'.

This rule—called here the 'time interval rule'—was evolved not specifically for financial business but for all business. It has always applied in finance because it has ensured that in the representative body the Crown's requests for money would have every chance of full and detailed consideration. Moreover, in days when communications were difficult it guarded against hasty, ill-considered, and unexpected decisions.

As early as 1510 Sir Thomas More acknowledged the significance of this procedure and even saw it to be appropriate for his 'Utopia': 'Furthermore, this custom also the council useth, to dispute or reason of no matter the same day that it is first proposed or put forth, but to defer it to the next sitting of the council.'[1] He saw wisdom in the cautionary approach. John Hooker, writing about 1568–71, explaining procedures for legislation, said that every bill 'must be read three several times, upon three several days'.[2] And when Clerk of the House, John Hatsell, described the proceedings of 1781, he could see that 'by this means due and sufficient notice of the subject should be given, and that members should not be surprised into a vote, but might come prepared to suggest every argument which the importance of the question may demand'.[3]

But, important though it is, even today the rule is not to be found generally expressed amongst the Standing Orders of the House; nor will it be found in any resolution of the House. There is one Standing Order that ensures its application at a particular point in financial proceedings. This is the reference contained in that procedural resolution of 1667 which, since 1852, has had Standing

1. Thomas More, *Utopia*—'Of the Magistrates'.
2. Quoted by E. and A. G. Porritt, *The Unreformed House of Commons* (CUP, 1909), p. 530.
3. Hatsell, *op. cit.*, vol III, p. 176.

Order authority. The relative section of the Order (at present No. 87) reads:

> If any motion be made in the House for any aid, grant or charge upon the public revenue, whether payable out of the Consolidated Fund or out of money to be provided by Parliament, or for any charge upon the people, the consideration and debate thereof shall not be presently entered upon, but shall be adjourned till such further day as the House shall think fit to appoint . . .

There is, therefore, a written prescription of an interval of time between the proposal of a charge in the House and its preliminary consideration in a Committee of the Whole. But for all other stages the necessity for time delays is based solely upon practice. There are, however, dispensations. Standing Orders have been used to discard the rule permanently in some of its applications; and in cases of special or urgent need it has sometimes been temporarily suspended by the House's simple resolution. But it continues to have considerable procedural significance.

Jeremy Bentham devoted attention to the time-interval principle in his treatise on *Political Tactics*. He wrote about the procedure of giving three readings to a bill, to enable debate to be reiterated, with the stages separated by time delays. He held several advantages for the procedure—that it provided:

(i) Maturity of deliberation arising from the opportunities given to a greater number of persons.

(ii) Opportunity afforded to the public to make itself heard—and to members to consult enlightened persons out of doors.

(iii) Prevention of the effect of eloquence, by which an oration might obtain votes on a sudden impulse.

(iv) Protection of the minority of the assembly by securing to it different methods at which to state its opinions.

(v) Opportunity for members absent during the first debate to attend when they perceive their presence may influence the fate of the bill.[1]

1. Bentham, *op. cit.*, vol II, p. 360.

Bentham was apprehensive of an inert House; it has been said that the problem of his time 'was not to check the flow of oratory but to induce it to flow at all'. And it is significant that when Josef Redlich came from Austria to study the House's procedure at the end of the nineteenth century he saw Bentham's ideas on this practice to be dangerous. 'It never entered his [Bentham's] mind', he wrote, 'that there might be absolutely irreconcilable parties, which would only be spurred-on by defeat to fresh exertions, that there might be minorities who would never submit without trying every conceivable means of carrying their wishes into effect.' Redlich feared that repetitive stages in debate gave undue scope to militant minorities and refractory political groups to obstruct the business of government.

Bentham and Redlich were influenced by the political conditions in which they found the House of Commons. 'When Bentham wrote', said Redlich, 'the memory of fierce party antagonisms and religious struggles of the seventeenth century had long since faded away . . . the parties, notwithstanding their antagonism on certain questions, were filled with the same sentiment towards the state, and possessed it in the same degree.' Reiterated debate, Redlich claimed, if appropriate to Bentham's time, was inappropriate to his own.[1]

Redlich, on the other hand, was influenced by the turbulent political clashes of the eighties, when Irish intransigents exploited the procedures of the House. In those conditions provisions for reiterated debate were an expensive luxury. Significant here, however, is that the rule survived both political climates, and more significantly, it continues to survive—albeit with some declared modifications—even today. The purpose in this study is to measure the extent of the modifications, and the reality of the rule in present conditions. And this can be done as part of a closer examination of the House's methods for expenditure business (Chapter 3) and revenue business (Chapter 5).

---

1. Redlich, *op. cit.*, vol III, p. 192.

3

THE CONTROL OF EXPENDITURE
BY PARLIAMENTARY DEBATE

There is no precise definition of the extent or the means for parliamentary control of expenditure in Britain. In theory control is absolute, but in practice it is slight. Lord Kennet expressed the theory in his *System of National Finance*. He claimed: '. . . every penny that is collected and every penny that is spent is collected and spent under the authority of some Act of Parliament, permanent or temporary. In the matter and manner of getting and spending the Executive is wholly subject to Parliament and has no power to move a hair's breadth beyond the powers which Parliament entrusts to it.'[1] Mr E. A. (later Sir Edward) Fellowes (Clerk of the House of Commons 1955–62), as long ago as 1925, expressed the practice. He asserted that it is now '. . . an anachronism to talk of the control of Parliament over finance: the control is that of the House of Commons alone'. And then he added: '. . . to talk of the power of the House of Commons is almost as misleading, for it has little power against the government.'[2] Where, then, is the truth?

Obviously, if the dialectic about representative control of public expenditure is to be fruitful, there must be some agreement about what control actually means. It is true that every expenditure and

1. E. Hilton Young (Lord Kennet), *The System of National Finance* (third edition, John Murray, 1936), p. 3.

2. J. W. Hills and E. A. Fellowes, *The Finance of Government* (second edition, Philip Allen, 1932), p. 8.

tax proposal must be authorised by an Act of Parliament to be effective. This means then that the Parliament's financial control is synonymous with its control over legislation. Indeed, it should be tighter than that because all financial proposals are accorded that special 'preliminary' stage for detailed scrutiny in the Committee of the Whole House. Control, from the institutional viewpoint, therefore, looks to be infinite. Kennet, it seems, is right.

But if the Executive has a monopoly over the initiation of expenditure (and taxing) proposals in the House, and uses this, as it does at present, to the extent of more than £7,000 millions per year, and if at the same time it demands an unqualified acceptance of its proposals through the use of its majority, by sanctions based on party discipline, and by using threats of governmental resignation if defeated—even on the smallest item—what of control then? Obviously, if the House has little power against the Government, Fellowes is right.

There will always be disputation about the deficiencies or the excesses of control—especially financial control—exercised by representative bodies. And in the United Kingdom, where the intricate procedures of the House of Commons prompt a Kennet-type interpretation, and the House's record of achievement a Fellowes conclusion, there is naturally some confusion.

Where, then, does a study of expenditure control start? Obviously, it is necessary to separate myth from reality—the dignified from the efficient elements of the control process. In general, the four financial rules nowadays look like Bagehot's 'dignified' parts, and they will first command attention. To see the development of 'efficient' elements it is necessary to look to the newer methods of the House, so far unexplained here, but which have increasing significance. These are the select committees with financial responsibilities, viz. the Committee of Public Accounts, the Estimates Committee, and the Select Committee on Nationalised Industries.[1] They will be considered together in Chapter 4.

---

1. A peculiar quirk in 'House of Commons language' is the omission of the prefix 'Select Committee' when reference is made to a committee established under authority of a Standing Order.

The Committee of Supply

The Committee of Supply is the principal 'dignified' organ of the House of Commons in expenditure control. Redlich, at the turn of the century, saw it as '. . . the apparatus whereby the House . . . makes effective its absolute control over the whole of the administration of national and industrial finance'.[1] Set up early in every session, its terms of reference are 'to consider of the supply to be granted to Her Majesty', and its procedures, still explained to the last detail in a forty-page chapter of Erskine May, are based upon Rule 2's presumption of prior parliamentary scrutiny of every Executive expenditure proposal, however detailed, before legal approval. Whilst the basic form of the committee is of seventeenth-century origin, most of its procedures and precedents are from the House's early-nineteenth-century endeavours to restrain public expenditure.

Supply, however, does not embrace all governmental expenditure. The Committee of Supply's functions have never been as comprehensive as Redlich asserted. Some services of government are financed permanently, by statute, and the Executive needs no further parliamentary authority for them. These, known as Consolidated Fund Services, comprise about 10 per cent of total departmental needs. They include expenditures such as those for the service of the national debt, the civil list, the salaries of judges and the Speaker. They are charges upon the public revenue that have been removed from politics; and the scope of the annual expenditure review in the Committee of Supply is reduced accordingly. Furthermore, it should be emphasised the Supply grants are exclusive of the wide range of local authorities' spending, and most of the expenditure of the nationalised industries.

The 'dignified' momentum gathers annually when the Queen, in her speech from the throne at the opening of every session, directs words exclusively to the few assembled commoners standing at the Bar of the House of Lords—'Members of the House of Commons—Estimates for the coming year will be laid before you

1. Redlich, *op. cit.*, vol III, p. 136.

in due course'. This royal reference to Estimates, interpreted by purists as 'The Financial Initiative of the Crown' (Rule 1), initiates a whole host of Supply demands. These emerge throughout the year in the form of Civil Estimates, Defence Estimates, Revised Estimates, Supplementary Estimates (once thought to defeat the whole financial system but which nowadays are almost seasonal), Votes on Account and Excess Grants. They are all the result of months of administrative preparation in both the Treasury and other departments, and collectively they represent a compromise between the principle of strictly annual cash accounting and the necessity to have the Executive constantly supplied with funds to meet fluctuating expenditure needs.

The Treasury claims a Utopian function for the Estimates. Their purpose, they say, is 'for Parliamentary, Treasury and Departmental control of expenditure; for helping each Department's financial management; for analysis of the national economy; and for public understanding of Government expenditure'.[1] Possibly, politicians are more realistic. A Chief Secretary of the Treasury (Henry Brooke), speaking of his mind rather than his hand, once said: '. . . the whole task of government is so vast nowadays and the figures so big, they [the Estimates] are almost ungraspable.'[2] But whatever their purpose, and size, all the Estimates documents, upon receipt by the House, are formally referred to the Committee of Supply.

If the Estimates are 'ungraspable' there is no doubt that the procedures of the Committee of Supply for their consideration presume otherwise. Their basic procedural premise is 'that the charge shall be made as easy upon the people as possible'.[3] The committee's methods presuppose their complete and thorough scrutiny and, if necessary, their reduction by the whole House, prior to being granted.

The whole range of Supply procedures came under review a

1. HC 184 (Session 1960–1), p. 1.
2. 652 HC Deb., 5s., c. 223.
3. Erskine May, *Parliamentary Practice* (first edition, 1844), p. 332.

E

century ago (in 1857) upon the appointment of a committee 'to consider the present forms for the conduct of Public Business in Committee of Supply'.[1] As a result of those investigations, the House, in 1858, and again in 1868, adopted long and detailed resolutions declaring Supply methods. These, in theory, still apply. They provide:

That when a motion is made in Committee of Supply, to omit or reduce any item of a vote, a question shall be proposed from the Chair for omitting or reducing such item accordingly; and members shall speak to such question only, until it has been disposed of.

That when several motions are offered, they shall be taken in the order in which the items to which they relate appear in the printed estimates.

That after a question has been proposed from the Chair for omitting or reducing any item, no motion shall be made, or debate allowed, upon any preceding item.

That when it has been proposed to omit or reduce items in a vote, the question shall be afterwards put upon the original vote, or upon the reduced vote, as the case may be.

That after a question has been proposed from the Chair for a reduction of the whole vote, no motion shall be made for omitting or reducing any item.[2]

These were the procedures for 'saving candle ends'; they provided for the committee's scrutiny to be narrowed to the smallest Estimates' item. In defending them in 1888 the Clerk of the House told a select committee that 'The great advantage of putting the reduction of the item, is that debate is immediately confined to that item and you get a debate concentrated on and restricted to one point. If you move to reduce the whole Vote there is not of course the same limitation to the debate to a particular subject.'[3]

But whether members in fact wished to use the Supply debates for their intended purpose was another matter. Dicey wrote of 'collectivism' and the 'socialistic legislation' that brought a new

1. HC 261 (Session 1857 (2)).   2. CJ (1858) 113; *ibid* (1868) 145.
3 Sir Reginald Palgrave, HC 281 (Session 1888), Q. 458.

political atmosphere to the nineteenth-century House of Commons. There was a new and growing urge for the extension of the authority of the State accompanied by plans for increased expenditure. 'Peace and retrenchment', the canons of political action at the beginning of the century, were replaced by cries for social justice and the alleviation of poverty.[1] As Sir Gilbert Campion put it, 'when social reform became the dominant interest the representatives of the people ceased to be a check and began to apply the spur to [public] expenditure'.[2] In this new environment the procedural framework of the Committee of Supply became inappropriate. Yet it was retained—and, significantly, it continues to be retained, even today.

In the latter part of the nineteenth century the Supply process became obviously artificial. It was confusing to many members, and also frustrating. The verbal rulings and the frequent admonitions of chairmen, seeking to preserve the committee's pure financial purpose, were but frail restraints against the persistence of members with expanding electorates to please. Members preferred to comment on the Government's policy, or suggest new policy, rather than to discuss the financial minutiae of public administration.

In this perplexing climate for deliberation the principal restriction imposed upon members was the increasingly restrictive application of the rule of the financial initiative of the Crown. Whilst social reforms increasingly called for expanded expenditure, rulings were given that no amendment proposal was acceptable if it would have that effect.[3] If members proposed to increase expenditure on any item or vote they had to formulate their amendment as a motion that sought its decrease. This procedural hypocrisy has by now become well known—the Estimates may be reduced, but not increased, except on the initiative of a Minister. But that was not the only restriction. The chagrin of members was aggravated by the

---

1. H. V. Dicey, *Lectures on the Relations Between Law and Public Opinion in England during the nineteenth century* (Macmillan, 1905), pp. 302 and 409–11.

2. HC 189-I (Session 1945–6), p. xxiv.

3. See precedents cited by Erskine May, *Parliamentary Practice* (seventeenth edition, 1964), pp. 759–62.

imposition of a qualitative restriction upon what members actually said in debate. There were necessary rules of relevance, but even when they were observed members were not permitted to refer in Supply debate to the need for new legislation; and with members' attitudes becoming sympathetic towards extending the functions of the State, this became increasingly repressive. The restriction was defended by the Clerk Assistant of the House in 1876 on the grounds that the House 'acting as the dispenser of Parliamentary aids, acts solely as a controlling authority; the sole power of the Committee of Supply, both in theory and practice, is restrictive not initiative'.[1] Attempts are still made to justify the limitation on that ground.

Many studies of the House of Commons of the nineteenth century have referred to the changing nature of Supply debates. A. V. Dicey thought the changes were evident between 1820 and 1850, and he referred to Joseph Hume's indefatigable efforts to secure economy. These he claimed were received with 'as much derision as admiration'.[2] Walter Bagehot, writing of debates pre-1867, referred to a belief that 'if you want to raise a certain cheer in the House of Commons make a general panegryic on economy; if you want to invite a sure defeat, propose a particular saving'.[3] And Thomas Erskine May, writing of the membership of the House of Commons in the 1860's, suggested that 'so far from opposing the demands of the Crown, they have rather laid themselves open to the charge of too facile an acquiescence in a constantly increasing expenditure'.[4]

By 1888 a Select Committee on Financial Procedure was prepared to admit a trace of failure in the whole granting process. Set up 'to consider the procedure by which the House annually granted Supplies to Her Majesty', the committee agreed that 'the actual reductions of the Votes by the Committee of Supply had apparently been slight in proportion to the amount of parliamentary time occupied in the consideration of the Estimates'. But it went on to express the belief that 'They had no doubt that discussion in the

1. Sir Reginald Palgrave, *Quarterly Review*, vol 141, *op. cit.*, p. 228.
2. Dicey, *op. cit.*, p. 302 and 411 (fn. 2).   3. Bagehot, *op. cit.*, p. 154.
4. T. Erskine May, *Constitutional History of England*, *op. cit.*, vol II, p. 100.

Committee of Supply has had a considerable effect in preventing increase of expenditure'. The significant feature of the 1888 enquiry was the Committee's acknowledgement of the irrepressible tendency in Supply debate for members to discuss policy issues rather than financial details. Yet it was not condoned.[1] 'Large political and theoretical issues', said the Clerk of the House in evidence, '. . . are foreign to the matter which the committee has to consider, viz. the economic use and application of the money which is being granted by the House of Commons.'[2] Greater realism, however, came from the Clerk Assistant (A. J. Milman); he claimed: 'since the Reform Act of 1867 matters have been very much more discussed than they were before'. And, he asserted, 'you cannot prevent questions being raised and debate arising which involve the policy of the vote as well as the financial fitness of the vote; . . . it is impossible to prevent debate other than mere economical debate'.[3] But the select committee, in reporting, was equivocal. Discussion on policy, it suggested, was 'a valuable and useful privilege . . . although these questions . . . may not always be raised in the most convenient or useful form, and may be complicated by much irrelevant and unimportant matter. . . .'[4]

In spite of obvious difficulties and the incongruous features of Supply debates each session, it was not until 1896 that action was taken. Conservative Leader of the House Mr Arthur Balfour, dissatisfied with the House's dilatoriness in its annual approval of Estimates, and shunning the politics of a preliminary enquiry by select committee, proposed firm limitations on the length of Estimates debates. He justified the move with:

Many hon. Gentlemen have a kind of hazy notion that the object of discussion in Supply is to ensure an economical administration of public money on the part of the Government. This is, I believe, an ancient and deeply rooted superstition, and it is a superstition that has absolutely no justification in the existing circumstances of Parliamentary Government. . . . In my opinion the discussion in Supply fulfils a function even more

1. HC 281 (Session 1888), p. iii.
2. Sir Reginald Palgrave, *ibid*, Q. 377, 428.
3 *ibid*, Q. 445.   4. *ibid*, p. iii.

important than it did in the days of Hume when the object was in the main criticism of expenditure rather than policy. For now, broadly Supply alone affords private Members in this House the right of criticism, that constant power of demanding from the Government explanations of their administrative and executive action. . . .While Supply does not exist for the purpose of enforcing economy on the Government, it does exist for the purpose of criticising the policy of the Government, of controlling their administration, and bringing them to book for their policy at home and abroad.[1]

This was an admirable exposition of the modern function of the Committee of Supply. The procedure of the committee implied one thing—economic scrutiny; the trend of debates favoured another—discussion of political issues. Balfour sought to sweep away all inhibitions restraining members from the overt use of Supply procedures for political polemics. He took the average of the number of days devoted to Supply in the preceding six years (1890–5) and proposed that that average—twenty sitting days—be allotted annually for the new purpose. But he added an important proviso—that the twenty allotted days were to be taken each year before the 5 August when the Estimates would be put to the vote (the House, said Balfour, 'is not in its best Parliamentary form' after August bank holiday). This was simply the adaptation of the 'guillotine' procedure—first adopted in 1887—to Supply business. It assured the Government that the final vote on its expenditure budget would not be unduly delayed. The new procedure was given a period of trial, and in 1902 it was finally incorporated in the Standing Orders of the House. But in spite of Balfour's statement of the new purpose of Supply debates there was no written declaration; that, unfortunately, was left to chance, and further confusion. For almost half a century successive select committees enquiring into the financial procedures laboured under the premise that the function of the Supply Committee remained one of detailed financial scrutiny; and from decade to decade they stumbled upon the realities of Supply debate, and announced them dramatically, as if they had split the atom.

1. XXXVII, HC Deb., 4s., cc. 723–6.

Select committees of enquiry reporting on questions of financial procedure in 1903, 1918, and 1931–2 were strongly critical of the methods of the House for the scrutiny and grant of expenditure Estimates. They all reported in the vein that the Committee of Supply 'was a very imperfect instrument for the control of expenditure'; that it 'was ill equipped for enquiry'; that it 'has the name but none of the methods of a committee'; that it was 'hardly the instrument to achieve a close and exhaustive examination of the immense and complex estimates'; and one committee alleged (1918) that 'if the estimates were never presented, and the Committee ot Supply never set up there would be no noticeable difference'.[1] If was not until 1945–6 that a Select Committee on Procedure began its enquiry with a Balfour-type understanding of the Committee of Supply as its starting point:

The passing of the Estimates in the Committee of Supply is the formal procedure by which the expenditure of Departments is authorised, but, as is well known, this procedure has almost ceased to serve the purpose of financial scrutiny and is used almost exclusively for the criticism of policy and administration.[2]

That was a hopeful sign, but, notwithstanding it, the confusion has continued. Many people, some in ignorance, some by design, have harboured nostalgia for the financial ways of the early nineteenth century. The Leader of the House (R. A. Butler) told a Select Committee on Procedure in 1959 that 'one of the weaknesses of the pressure of work in Parliament is that we do not in fact spend enough time on examining Estimates'.[3] The so-called Hinchingbrooke Revolt in 1960 was based on Conservative back-bench dissatisfaction with the inevitable practice of voting Estimates 'on the nod'. And Dr Paul Einzig's recent study of *The Control of the Purse* (1959) questioned '. . . why the limited amount of time available for the consideration of supply grants should not be devoted

1. HC 242 (Session 1903); HC 121 (Session 1918); and HC 129 (Session 1931–2).
2. HC 189–1 (Session 1945–6), para. 36.
3. HC 92–1 (Session 1958–9), Q. 1102.

to the scrutiny of as many votes as could receive attention within the limited number of days'.[1]

The conflicting attitudes of realists and romanticists in this subject have contributed a confusing picture. Indeed, it was not until the fourteenth edition of Erskine May's *Parliamentary Practice* (1946) that the first mention was made in that work, albeit briefly, of any change in the function of the Committee of Supply. And except for that fleeting digression, May's chapter on Supply, even in later editions, has continued to presume that the nineteenth-century function of the committee is the twentieth-century norm.[2]

Why is it, then, that in the face of repeated complaints the old Supply Committee, and its methods, have been retained? Possibly the availability of the Estimates Committee since 1912, and a Select Committee on Nationalised Industries since 1956, have lessened member dissatisfaction. But a greater possibility is that the old Supply procedures offer advantages to the front benches on both sides that are too important to be discarded lightly.

When examined closely it becomes evident that the methods of the Committee of Supply act in restraint of politics. Designed to impose economic restraints on governments via parliamentary debate, they have been converted to impose political restraints on the House. The essence of every motion that comes before the committee is cash—a typical motion would be:

That a further sum not exceeding £—— millions be granted to Her Majesty for services connected with Education in Scotland.

As May puts it, debate 'must be kept to the specific object which is placed before the committee'; 'the Committee of Supply cannot attach a condition or an expression of opinion to a grant or alter its destination'; and each motion 'can only be dealt with by being

---

1. Einzig, *op. cit.*, p. 329. (See also the cry of Labour's disillusioned Mr Robert Maxwell, on 16 December 1964—704 HC Deb., 5s., cc. 393–400.)

2. This dilatory acknowledgement of fact had a profound influence in retarding an enlightened development of financial control in 'Dominions' such as Canada and Australia.

agreed to, reduced, negatived, suspended or, by leave, withdrawn'. For example, no amendment motion, expressing modification of the policy that a particular vote embraces, would be acceptable. All amendments must relate to pounds, shillings, and pence. May's Supply chapter sets forth restriction after restriction aimed at keeping Supply debate strictly to financial objectives.[1] Possibly the Committee of the Whole House was John Eliot's way to the truth in the seventeenth century, but if a member in the twentieth century martyred himself in the Supply cause his sanity would be questioned.

Furthermore, there is the restriction on members in the prohibition of reference to the need for new legislation. This is based on the assumption that Supply debate is purely financial. In 1945 a government spokesman told a Select Committee on Procedure that a relaxation of this limitation 'would greatly increase the burden of the Ministers and their departments in preparing for these debates and frequently give rise to pressure for statements on matters which were still under consideration by the Government and might well be at the moment the subject of delicate negotiations'.[2] And in 1958 Mr Speaker Morrison supported the proscription by reasoning: 'If you propose to change by law you should remedy your grievance by bill. . . . Legislation is too important a matter to be introduced adventitiously into the discussion. . . .'[3] And that still holds.

Much has been made in numerous studies of the House of Commons of the concession granted the official Opposition on allotted Supply days permitting them the choice of the subject of debate. (Nowadays the 'allotted' days have been increased from Balfour's twenty to twenty-six per session—approximately one-sixth of the House's sitting days.) Whether the concession was part of the 1896 Balfour bargain is not clear, but it began soon afterwards. Erskine May acknowledged the custom as 'not strictly a rule, or enforceable by the Chair, but a convention dependent only on the respect which every Government feels for the rights of minorities and the corporate

1. May, *op. cit.* (seventeenth edition, 1964), pp. 735–76.
2. HC 189-1, Q.Q. 1864, 3449, 5840.   3. HC 92-1, Q.Q. 908-9.

sense of the House'. It is not part of the Standing Orders, and May went so far as to say 'whether [it is] strictly part of the procedure may be doubted'.[1]

'Respect for the rights . . .', etc., sound altruistic. But are the benefits in one direction only? Although the Opposition chooses the subject of debate on a Supply day, the Government front bench remains in control, and not only as a result of its strength in the division lobbies. As the debates are held in the Committee of Supply, the Opposition is limited by the artificial debating forms referred to above, and also to the moving of amendment motions that demand explanations that they do not mean what they say.[2] In this way the Government is protected from expressive amendment proposals that would require an immediate and reasoned decision on its own part. And, moreover, an allotted Supply day is a limited day, in that debate is terminated by Standing Order at 10 p.m.

It is true that arrangements are increasingly made on a Supply day, 'through the usual channels', to dispose of the formal financial question and conduct the debate in the House, on a reasoned motion, free from the Supply Committee's restraints on debate. But for this procedure approval is necessary, and the so-called Opposition right becomes conditional upon government (usually Leader of the House) agreement. It is normally given, but it could be withheld.

There is no doubt that the technicalities of the Supply granting process help to keep back-benchers below decks in finance. Their effect is that for twenty-six days of each session back-benchers have no rights of positive initiative. This, for example, was one of the frustrations of a Conservative 'Hinchingbrooke' revolutionary in 1960—'is all the initiative to be on the other side of the Committee', he asked, and then asserted 'some rights and privileges should

1. Erskine May, *Parliamentary Practice* (fifteenth edition, 1950), p. xlviii.
2. Take, for example, Mr James Callaghan in a debate on East and Central African Affairs in 1961. 'I beg to move, to leave out £3,671,010 and insert £3,670,010 instead thereo' . . . 'In case there should be any misunderstanding in the Committee let me say that the purpose of my amendment is not to aid the Chancellor in his new economies. In our view this is the very last field to which the Chancellor should turn to seek economies. . . .' (645 H C Deb., 5s., c. 239.)

repose with my honourable Friends and myself on the Government benches to initiate debate on specific Votes and supplementary Votes'.[1] From the Opposition side Labour back-bencher Sidney Silverman saw the artificial procedures being used as 'a general conspiracy between the two front benches to prevent a vote being taken at any time in connection with a specific issue'.[2] And in a different but relevant context Silverman claimed: 'It is true that there could be a vote at the end of the day, but nobody would know on what specific matter, or any specific matter, the vote would be apparent.'[3] And, as Labour back-bencher Leslie Hale put it, '. . . the usual channels select the matter for discussion . . . and the opportunity for discussing many controversial Estimates does not arise at all'.[4]

Procedures, therefore, as emphasised above, are instruments of control, and in the Supply process they have proved 'dignified' and singularly effective means in the hands of the party oligarchies for controlling their rank and file; and, more particularly, for controlling democratically elected representatives in the expenditure-granting process. This is seldom acknowledged by the advocates of abolition; nor do they suggest alternatives.

The Committee of Ways and Means

So far attention has been focussed on the Committee of Supply's procedures. There are, however, other opportunities for the consideration of the administrative and political implications of expenditure Estimates. But, like the Committee of Supply, they too have had their original purpose and efficacy curtailed.

There is the well-known step for approving, in the Committee of Ways and Means, the issue of moneys from the Consolidated Fund up to the limit of the grants made in the Committee of Supply. This is known as the 'spending' function of the Committee of Ways and Means. Alpheus Todd explained the nineteenth-century significance of this: 'The votes in committee of Supply authorise the expenditure; the votes in committee of Ways and Means provide

1. Mr Gerald Nabarro, 618 H C Deb., 5s., cc. 204–5.
2. 660 H C Deb., 5s., cc. 682–3.
3. 659 H C Deb., 5s., c. 1545.   4. 543 H C Deb., 5s., c. 1321.

the funds to meet the expenditure.'[1] In accordance with Sections 14
and 15 of the Exchequer and Audit Departments Act of 1866, the
Comptroller and Auditor-General has authority only to permit
issues of 'credits' to the Treasury 'not exceeding' the whole of the
Ways and Means granted by Parliament at the time. The political
implications of this procedure were emphasised by the Select
Committee on Public Moneys in 1857:

. . . although the House of Commons at an early part of the Session might
have voted the whole of the Supplies of the year, they could still hold their
constitutional check upon the Minister by limiting the grant of Ways and
Means to an amount sufficient only to last such time as they might think
proper to give him the means of carrying on the public service, and they
are by such grants at all times enabled to prevent the Minister from dissolv-
ing or proroguing Parliament.[2]

In the Committee of Supply, therefore, elected members, in
theory, exercise a veto over any of the details of the expenditure
plans, whereas in the Committee of Ways and Means their veto is
over a lump-sum grant.

The lump-sum veto has obvious importance from the viewpoint
of parliamentary control of the Executive. But members, domin-
ated by party, show no inclination to use it; it is a relic of the
classical era of responsible cabinet government. Yet its neglect did
not worry Sir Ralph Hawtrey who concluded:

Just because the power exists it does not require it to be exercised. A
government bows to a vote of want of confidence. But it must not be
concluded that the point of withholding Ways and Means, or the control
of the Exchequer on which that power depends, can be safely withdrawn.
Constitutional checks may remain in abeyance for generations, but that
does not mean that they are superfluous; they may be unchallenged simply
because they are decisive. . . . It is when some confusion of parties exists
that the sanction, by which a vote of want of confidence is enforceable,
becomes important.[3]

1. Alpheus Todd, On Parliamentary Government in England (Longmans, Green,
1892), vol II, p. 216.
2. HC 279 (Session 1857 (2)), pp. 26–7.   3. Hawtrey, op. cit., p. 24.

But there is every indication that the Ways and Means veto is now a museum-piece and that there would be difficulties in rehabilitating it. Although once a latent veto of importance, a Clerk of the House, Sir Edward Fellowes, has claimed it to be now 'undebatable'.[1] Erskine May's recent editions dismiss it with the curious rationalisation, 'As the amounts of ways and means resolutions follow automatically from the amounts of supply resolutions already voted, and as any alteration would involve inconsistency with previous decisions, no amendment of a ways and means resolution is in order except for the purpose of correcting an error.' And May contends further, that the stage is now 'purely formal' and gives rise to 'no debate'.[2] Adding to its critics, Sir William Anson saw the stage as 'a needless expenditure of Parliamentary time'[3] and Sir Ivor Jennings suggested that 'as it is pure form' nobody has bothered to abolish it.[4]

It would be easy to assert that this procedural step has lapsed simply because the House has not chosen to use it. But it goes deeper than that. Successive governments have become hypersensitive to the sanctions the House may exercise in approving their expenditure grants in legislation. They have frequently declared that every single step in the long and complex expenditure granting process is tantamount to a vote of want of confidence. They threaten that if defeated on any question, regardless of its financial significance, they will resign or seek a dissolution. In consequence, the Ways and Means veto, like any other step in the financial process, has become simply one of many vetos that could be applied by the House throughout the session. It has lost its relative importance.

Consolidated Fund Acts

The application of the third rule of financial procedure to the Supply process means that grants made formally each session by votes in the Committee of Supply and the Committee of Ways and

---

1. HC 92-1 (Session 1958–9), p. 12 and Q. 169.
2. May, *Parliamentary Practice* (seventeenth edition, 1964), pp. 770–1.
3. Anson, *op. cit.*, p. 278. 4. Jennings, *op. cit.*, p. 312.

Means must finally be embodied in legislation, and passed. This gives rise to two or three Consolidated Fund Bills each year and the annual Consolidated Fund (Appropriation) Bill. These, together, absorb about six sitting days per session.

The first reading of each of these bills, as with all proposed laws, is now accepted as a formality and is not debatable. The second and third reading stages afford opportunity for general debate, and in recognition of the historic power of the House in financial legislation they have not been included in the allotted day system. In this way they are exempted from the automatic adjournment of debate at 10 p.m. In recent years, however, governments have not been inhibited in using the closure procedure to bring debate on them to a peremptory end.[1] Theoretically, it is at the committee and report stages that details—in these cases financial details—are again thrown open for discussion. But a Standing Order (at present No. 40) prohibits '. . . a Consolidated Fund or an Appropriation Bill' being sent upstairs to the Standing Committees; such bills are retained in the Committee of the Whole House, where the Whip is strongest, and where all members may contribute to debate. But again there are procedural restraints on participation. The succession of restrictions imposed by the Chairman (Sir Gordon Touche) at the committee stage of a Consolidated Fund Bill in 1961 indicates the blend of authoritarianism and confusion that exists about members' contributions. Some of the limitations applied on that occasion were:

I must warn the honourable member that there are technical difficulties about debating this. Supply has already been voted by the House and the Committee cannot override or amend the decision of the House.

I am sorry to interrupt the honourable member but it is clearly laid down that expenditure cannot be discussed on this Clause.

I am afraid the honourable member has proposed an Amendment to the Bill and we cannot have an Amendment.

We are not voting the money now. It has been voted by the Committee of Ways and Means, and the House has approved that decision.[2]

1. HC 271 (Session 1962–3), p. 6.   2. 635 HC Deb., 5s., cc. 165–200.

'Restriction', therefore, is the theme of the whole Supply granting process. The control methods of the nineteenth century have been subtly inverted to control the controllers. In general, the procedures for the use of twenty-six allotted Supply days, plus the procedures for the enactment of the grants made in Consolidated Fund Bills, make for a confused pattern of behaviour. The sequence of events has been adequately explained elsewhere,[1] but at this point a diagrammatic outline may be helpful (see p. 81).

With the House giving twenty-six days' consideration to matters of Supply there has been an understandable impatience with the procedural rule (Rule 4) that requires the interposition of an interval of time of at least one sitting day between the subsequent legislative stages, as a precaution against hasty consideration. Yielding to this, the House in 1919 adopted a Standing Order (at present No. 89) permitting the suspension of the rule's application between the committee, report and third reading stages of each Consolidated Fund Bill. The House, under Executive pressure, normally exercises this concession and, in consequence, the opportunities for members to exercise the legislative power of the House in enacting Supply grants is curtailed accordingly. The pattern of behaviour for each such bill—introduced after resolutions in the Committee of Supply and the Committee of Ways and Means—is now as follows:

First reading (a formality)

TIME INTERVAL

Second reading

TIME INTERVAL

Committee stage (Committee of the Whole) ⎫
Report of committee   ⎬ S.O. No. 89.
Third reading   ⎭

1. See Eric Taylor, *The House of Commons at Work* (Pelican, fifth edition, 1963), pp. 193–228.

Further evasion of parliamentary scrutiny

As the processes of the House in scrutinising expenditure have become, or have been rendered, less effective (and, as will be seen below, the Estimates Committee now provides only a token scrutiny), then it is to the Government's advantage to include the financial requests for as much of its new expenditure planning as it can possibly manage, within the Estimates and their related documents.

If a government seeks legislative approval of its new expenditure policies outside the annual Estimates–Supply cycle it invites political fire. The result, therefore, has been a continuing parliamentary-Executive wrangle about the authorisation of new services through the Estimates, the Committee of Supply, and subsequent Consolidated Fund and Consolidated Fund (Appropriation) Acts. Back-benchers, however, in opposition to this trend, have been limited to exhortation, and the Executive have held the upper hand. The Estimates documents, the Executive claim (under Rule 1), are prepared and presented to the House on their initiative, and matters of content are in their hands; and with uncharacteristic fatalism Erskine May submits 'there is . . . no legal restraint on the discretion of the Crown in presenting an estimate, or on that part of Parliament in authorising the expenditure . . . in the Appropriation Act. . . . There have been cases too, in which the Appropriation Act has been used, not merely as a substitute for specific legislation, but to override the limits imposed by existing legislation.' And May continues: 'The Treasury . . . have justified the practice on grounds of emergency rather than principle.'[1]

In the Treasury mind, however, we live in times of constant emergency. It was interesting to see that its officials went unchallenged when they told the Select Committee on Estimates in 1962 that they now use supplementary estimates 'to provide for any change of policy involving additional expenditure' or for '. . . a completely new service, something which had not been foreseen at all when the original estimate was framed'.[2]

1. Erskine May (seventeenth edition, 1964), *op. cit.*, pp. 775–6.
2. HC 228 (Session 1962–3), p. 1 and Q. 10.

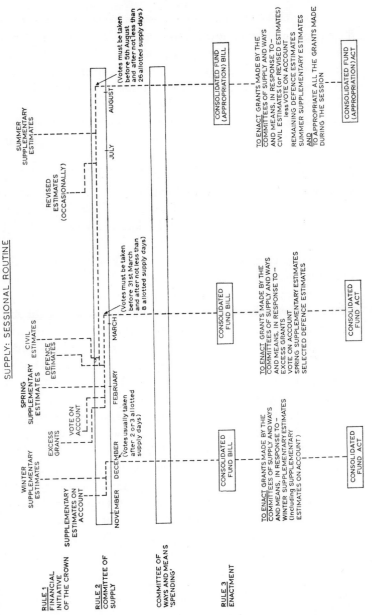

SUPPLY: SESSIONAL ROUTINE

Parliamentary control looks even weaker when we consider the discretion the Treasury now claims in its power of Virement. Since 1862 the Treasury has been given power in each annual Consolidated Fund (Appropriation) Act to switch expenditure between Service votes. And on civil votes the Treasury has claimed the discretion of authorising transfers of expenditure between subheads within votes. This has provided distinct administrative advantages. But now that some votes run at £50 millions and more, Virement, obviously, is a substantial power in the Executive's hands. And, furthermore, the Treasury asserts that they 'feel free to exercise a wide measure of discretion in this' and they use it 'to provide a new service "within the ambit" not foreseen when the estimate was presented'[1] and when 'we' think it 'does not raise matters of importance and interest to Parliament'.[2]

In addition to financing new services by Virement, there is the Civil Contingencies Fund. From this fund, Lord Bridges claims, 'the Treasury may authorise limited expenditure in advance of Parliamentary authority'.[3] This is as effective a method of by-passing prior parliamentary sanction of expenditure as could be imagined. The fund may be used to meet urgent and unforeseen expenditure, provide advances in respect of new services, or meet overspending on existing services, until such time as retrospective parliamentary approval is given and the fund is recouped.

In its present form the fund dates from 1862, and in its early years stood at only £120,000, but in 1913 it was increased to £300,000. From 1919 to 1921 'in very exceptional circumstances' it stood at £120 millions; and from 1921 to 1939 it was fixed at £1·5 millions—the normal peace-time figure. After the war (1946) it was put at £250·5 millions until 1950; then it was reduced to £126·5 millions and finally, in 1955, further reduced to its present figure, £75 millions—'or such lower amount as the Treasury may order'.[4] (This, however, is one discretionary power that the Treasury has not yet exercised.)

1. HC 251–1 (Session 1961–2), p. 471.   2. HC 41 (Session 1962–3), Q. 86.
3. Lord Bridges, *The Treasury* (Allen and Unwin, 1964), p. 33 fn.
4. See debate on Miscellaneous Financial Provisions Bill 1955—543 HC Deb., 5s., cc. 659–86.

The reduction of the fund in 1955 was a consequence of its abuse. The Conservative Government introduced legislation to effect the change after it was apparent that Mr Attlee's Government had used the fund to finance Britain's research and development of the atomic bomb without explicit and prior parliamentary approval; and had also used it in 1949 to make provisional advances of over £100 millions to finance deficits on the National Health Service until after the 1950 elections. And after 1955, in spite of its reduced size, it was equally convenient for financing provisionally any excesses in expenditure occasioned by the Conservative Government's agricultural support policies.[1]

Even at its reduced level the Civil Contingencies Fund gives the Executive substantial freedom from prior parliamentary scrutiny of its policy decisions. Now that Supplementary Estimates have become seasonal phenomena they may be used to provide several recoupments to the fund in the course of a financial year. In 1960–1, for example, it was recouped to the tune of £153 millions, and in 1961–2 £112 millions. This, obviously, is big business, which the representative body looks at, in its limited way, only retrospectively. Yet in 1963 the Comptroller and Auditor-General thought that even at its present level the fund gets the Treasury 'pretty tight up to the collar'.[2]

There is no doubt, therefore, that the Minister was right when he said Supply expenditure is 'ungraspable'. It shows no signs of diminishing. At the end of the next decade today's expenditure will seem of modest proportions.[3] The point to be made here is that the House of Commons does not control it in the way that its Supply procedures imply. These form a dignified façade for parliamentary activity which was probably never an adequate cover, but which in the mid-twentieth century is becoming increasingly threadbare.

1. Einzig, *op. cit.*, pp. 253–4; and HC 228 (Session 1962–3), p. 33.
2. HC 228 (Session 1962–3), Q. 272.
3. At the end of 1964 Labour's Chancellor of the Exchequer (James Callaghan) forecast: 'By 1968 the total expenditure will be £2,000 million more than it is today, without making allowances for increased prices in the interim.' 701, HC Deb., 5s., c. 1030.

It gives rise to confusion and disillusionment, particularly in circumstances where the methods have been adopted in new parliaments with filial respect; and it is sadly in need of reform. But before making reference to possible alternatives (Chapter 6) there is need to consider the special financial procedures devised for the House's approval of the expenditure provisions of those policies that must run the gauntlet of separate and specific statutory enactment—that is, policy bills and their associated money resolutions.

Money Resolutions

Mention has already been made of the political advantage for the Executive of including in the annual Estimates (and in the Supplementary Estimates) financial provision for as much of its policy arrangements, old and new, as it can manage. In this way, and with the help of the restrictive procedures of the Committee of Supply, interference by elected representatives is limited. But from time to time legal and political circumstances demand that express statutory authority be given to a new and particular policy involving expenditure. About one-third of the bills passed annually embody clauses that bring new and direct charges upon the public revenue, and which, in consequence of Rules 1 and 2, require special, 'preliminary', Committee of the Whole consideration. This is known as the Money Committee stage, from which emerges the Money Resolution.

The Money Resolution procedure, according to Lord Campion, is followed when a bill 'actually causes the issue out of the Exchequer of money which would not otherwise be issued, or places a liability on the Exchequer which would not otherwise accrue'.[1] It is, in fact, the resolution of a specially established Committee of the Whole—the Money Committee—and it determines the financial limits of a proposed law. That resolution, when adopted by the House, becomes the financial criterion to which all proposed amendments to the bill have to be matched.

In its origin (like all the committees created by Rule 2) the

1. Campion, *op. cit.*, p. 282.

Money Committee was devised in exercise of the House's financial autonomy and to provide scope for additional and particular scrutiny to the Crown's financial proposals. This was seen to be its role as late as 1937. When Sir Gilbert Campion was asked then to distinguish between a Money Committee and the Supply Committee, he answered:

I should think the great distinction really . . . is that Supply is old expenditure, whereas a Money Resolution is new expenditure and requires legislation, and the House, being a legislative body, would naturally expect more freedom on a matter which required legislation than upon a matter which was, like Supply, purely administration.[1]

Supply, however, is no longer solely 'old' expenditure. But the crux of Campion's distinction is that Supply grants, although embodied in legislation, are expressed in figures. Whereas policy legislation is different, it is in prose (albeit legal) and elected representatives aspire more to be masters of words than masters of figures; they claim the power to shape policy bills, and the Money Resolution procedure is designed to meet their aspiration. In theory it permits the reasoned determination by members of the financial scope of those clauses of bills that have financial implications.

But, as with Supply procedure, the Money Resolution has been inverted to become a technique by which the Executive may determine the limits of amendment permissible in the legislative process. It is now a means for the Executive control of the Commons, rather than the reverse. If its inversion was not evident to Campion in 1937, then it had made its mark upon him by 1945. He then defined the Money Resolution as:

. . . a neat and flexible instrument which can be nicely adjusted so as to allow the House just as much latitude in the criticism and amendment of the financial provisions of a bill as Ministers think reasonable.[2]

To judge the efficacy of Money Resolutions in modern conditions it is necessary to reflect on the role of the House of Commons

1. HC 149 (Session 1936–7), Q. 1470.   2. HC 189–1 (Session 1945–6), p. xxvii.

in legislation. This is a fundamental question usually overlooked in the wider issue of parliamentary reform. If we agree with R. A. Butler in his call to his contemporaries, '. . . we have to be, and must be, a legislative assembly . . .',[1] then the Money Resolution may be seen as a potential restriction upon the legislative freedom of the representative body. But if the role of the House of Commons is simply to rubber-stamp the Executive's proposals in legislation, then the procedure is admirable as a technique for keeping elected representatives, and the official Opposition, at bay for a major and important part of the legislative process.

The Executive's realisation of the power implicit in Money Resolutions came after the First World War. Until then the drafting of the motion to which the Crown's recommendation was signified (Rule 1), and which was the basis of the Money Resolution, was a function of the House's own officials. Through the use of general (non-specific) expressions they preserved for the House what they considered was a fair degree of amending freedom. But on 8 December 1919, as part of the procedural changes deemed necessary to meet the needs of post-war reconstruction, and after a Committee of the House had embarrassed the Government by amending the annual expenditure estimates by £4,800 (the case of the Lord Chancellor's bath),[2] Mr Speaker Lowther was advised by the Financial Secretary to the Treasury, Stanley Baldwin, in the following terms:

I am directed by the Lords Commissioners of His Majesty's Treasury to inform you that His Majesty's Government have decided that in future all Financial Resolutions for Bills should be placed on the Paper in the name of the Financial Secretary to the Treasury, and for that purpose Departments should be requested to submit the terms of Resolutions for Bills in which they are interested to the Treasury for the approval of the Financial Secretary before they are placed on the Paper.

Unlike some of his illustrious predecessors the Speaker submitted quietly to this Executive pressure. He endorsed the minute: 'I

1. 617 HC Deb., 5s., c. 37.   2. 118 HC Deb., 5s., c. 2323.

authorise the Public Bill Office to carry out the procedure above mentioned accordingly.'[1]

This was a major procedural take-over by the Executive. No doubt it could be justified on the analogy that as the Executive did, in fact, determine the form and the content of the Estimates, they should also determine the financial limits of proposed laws. But the fact that the instruction was tantamount to an Executive claim to legislative power took many years to penetrate.

The Financial Secretary's letter of 1919 had followed an intensive review of financial procedures by the Select Committee on National Expenditure in 1918. Twenty-six witnesses (including Sidney Webb and Sir Courtenay Ilbert) had been asked whether the Money Resolution should be abolished, and only two had replied in the affirmative. There was substantial support for the procedure on the premise of parliamentary sovereignty. The Money Resolution, it was agreed:

(i) Acts as a substantial check on expenditure owing to the reluctance of a Minister to face the discussion in Committee and on Report.

(ii) That it is essential for the purpose of maintaining ministerial responsibility and initiative in matters of finance.

(iii) It secures a separate discussion of the financial aspects of a bill which otherwise might be lost sight of.[2]

The committee concluded that the procedure 'serves a useful purpose but its utility could be further increased'. This, presumably, was the development that the Government feared most—hence the Treasury's communication with the Speaker.

The full realisation by members of the House of the power of the written word in Money Resolutions came in 1922. The Deputy Chairman of Ways and Means (Sir Edward Cornewell Lewis), on the Unemployment Insurance Bill, gave a ruling to indicate that the scope both for amendment proposals and for debate on the bill was in fact determined by the relevant Minister of the Crown and

1. HC 149 (Session 1936–7), p. 176.   2. HC 121 (Session 1918), p. 123.

the Financial Secretary to the Treasury when they agreed upon the proposed Money Resolution.[1] This subsequently became hard for members to swallow. Unlike previous quantitative restraints on their use of the time of the House, it brought a qualitative imposition upon their deliberative and legislative freedom. The words in the Money Resolution became of first importance, and there were strong objections.

In the mounting volume of social legislation presented to the Commons in the 1920–30's the freedom for members to move amendments became increasingly restricted. As one member recalled, 'the Departments began to realise that a new power had come into their hands'.[2] The restrictions imposed in the consideration of the Unemployed Insurance Bill 1933, the Depressed Areas (Development and Improvement) Bill 1934, the Education Bill 1936, and the Tithe Bill 1936 provoked widespread dissatisfaction. In 1934 Mr Speaker Fitzroy had occasion to express his concern at the trend: '. . . not only has the limit been reached but that it has been rather exceeded in the amount of detail which is put into Money Resolutions'.[3] And in 1937 H. B. Lees Smith, the Opposition's acknowledged expert on financial procedures, asserted that financial resolutions were '. . . tightened up, out of a desire on the part of civil servants to help their Ministers'.[4]

It was in March 1937 that Opposition patience expired. After the Government, via a Money Resolution, had imposed stringent limits on the amendment moving freedom of members in the passage of a Development and Improvement of Special Areas Bill, precluding the Opposition from proposing alternative areas for relief, the Leader, Mr Attlee, moved for the abolition of a Standing Order of 1919 origin, which was relevant to, but was not really the essence of, the problem. Apparently forced into this action by backbenchers, Mr Attlee emphasised that he had no intention of questioning the rule of the financial initiative of the Crown (Rule 1)

1. 152 HC Deb., 5s., c. 1588; and see HC 149 (Session 1936–7), p. vi.
2. Rt. Hon. H. B. Lees Smith, 321 HC Deb., 5s., c. 919.
3. 295 HC Deb., 5s., c. 1236.   4. 321 HC Deb., 5s., c. 922.

but launched a special debate on Money Resolutions. The debate ran for seven hours and it gave classic expression to the procedural dilemma of the time, viz. the demands of the Government to govern, and the demands of the elected representatives to be legislators.

Although hopelessly outnumbered, Mr Attlee fought the good fight. The Money Resolutions, he asserted, had '. . . become a weapon of the Executive against the legislature'. His motion, he said, although 'a technical matter of procedure', was really concerned with the question 'as to whether we have an opportunity, a full opportunity, of amending legislation'.[1]

The debate brought contributions from the Prime Minister (Mr Baldwin), Mr Aneurin Bevan, Mr Lloyd George, Mr Lees Smith, and the Attorney-General (Sir Donald Somerville). But it was Aneurin Bevan, from the back bench, who made the deepest penetration of the procedural fog. 'I sometimes get rather tired', he complained, 'of the indirectness of Parliamentary language which merely serves to obscure the real issue.' The Prime Minister's defence of the procedure, Bevan said, 'means that the Chancellor of the Exchequer must be hedged around with complicated Standing Orders in order to prevent Members of Parliament from getting at him'. And facetiously he added: 'the procedure of the House of Commons is now being changed in order to protect the Member of Parliament against the pressure of his own poor constituents'.[2]

The outcome of Mr Attlee's 1937 debate was the creation of a Select Committee on Procedure to consider specifically the problem of Money Resolutions. In spite of the government majority in its membership, the committee's terms of reference restricted it 'to the unimpaired maintenance of the principles embodied in [what were] Standing Orders Nos. 66 to 68' (that is, Rules Nos. 1 and 2). The committee took extensive evidence from parliamentarians and officials, and consideration was given to the idea of a further Standing Order to prohibit restrictive Money Resolutions. That, however, received short shrift on the ground that 'it is not part of

1. 321 HC Deb., 5s., cc. 815–16.   2. *ibid*, cc. 849–50.

the Committee's intention to propose any innovation in practice. . .'.

In a little more than two months the committee produced a report characterised by the intensity of its enquiry and the timidity of its findings. Its principal recommendation was for a declaratory resolution by the House exhorting Executive tolerance and Money Resolutions that would not restrict unduly the control which the House 'has been accustomed to exercise over legislation'. The report also proposed that the 'Speaker should be judge of whether any particular financial resolution complied with the declaration of the House'.[1]

The Prime Minister, however, subsequently insisted that the committee's recommendation for a declaratory resolution would be incompatible with the principle of the financial initiative of the Crown, which, he said, 'the Government considered of supreme importance'. The Speaker, on the side of authority, backed the Prime Minister. He feared the consequences of being umpire of Money Resolutions and claimed: 'In these matters it is essential to look ahead, and the time might come, especially if it is to become a practice to oppose the Speaker in his constituency at Election times, that such a ruling might be referred to . . .'.[2] The Prime Minister and the Speaker won the day. The former, in place of the recommended Commons' declaration, arranged a compromise solution. Written instructions were sent to all departments and to all Parliamentary Counsel, insisting, *inter alia*:

. . . it is the definite intention of His Majesty's government to secure that financial resolutions in respect of Bills shall be so framed as not to restrict the scope within which the Committee on the Bills may consider amendments further than is necessary to enable the Government to discharge their responsibilities in regard to public expenditure. . . .[3]

The House was informed of the instructions but no member took the point that they were declaratory of 'Executive' rather than 'Parliamentary' control of finance.

1. HC 149 (Session 1936–7). This report provides the most penetrating examination of the Money Resolutions procedure yet undertaken.
2. *ibid*, p. 175.   3. 328 HC Deb., 5s., c. 1595.

The problem of Money Resolutions has lingered on, and in the quarter-century since 1937 repeated objections have been voiced against the restrictions they have brought to the legislative process.[1] They came to the political surface again in 1956 with an Opposition plea for tolerance on grounds 'You will not get freedom or democracy in this country by trussing the Opposition inside Money Resolutions'.[2] On that occasion R. A. Butler, as Leader of the House, defended the trend with: 'It is always difficult for a Government to draw up Money Resolutions to suit themselves, the House of Commons and the cause of liberty. . . .'[3] Butler was troubled by the difficulty of pleasing all the members all the time and his statement as much as defined the Executive's order of priorities in the legislative process. Once again back-benchers were not persuaded, and yet another Select Committee on Procedure emerged with Money Resolutions included in its terms of reference.

At the 1956 enquiry the Government's sensitivity about financial responsibility again made reform in favour of the House virtually impossible. The Select Committee found 'justification for the feeling among certain members that money resolutions are, on certain occasions, drafted in an unduly restrictive way', and that 'Governments tend to err on the side of strictness'. But the committee did not stay long on the side of the angels; it denied strength to its case by asserting that the principle implicit in Standing Order No. 82 (Rule 1) was 'of fundamental constitutional importance', and it did not, therefore, wish to recommend change.[4]

In subsequent years, however, there has been less dissatisfaction with Money Resolutions. In 1959 the Clerk of the House told the Select Committee on Procedure that '. . . the ordinary run of money resolutions are now extremely widely drawn'.[5] And in 1965 the Clerk Assistant claimed 'the practical effect . . . of the money resolution procedure is not, as is so often supposed, to restrict the

---

1. See particularly Coal Industry Bill 1946 (418 HC Deb., 5s., cc. 982–1074); and Slum Clearance Bill 1956 (552 HC Deb., 5s., cc. 2328–54).
2. G. Mitchison, 522 HC Deb., 5s., c. 2336.
3. *ibid*, c. 2346.   4. HC 110 (Session 1956–7), p. v.
5. Sir Edward Fellowes, HC 92–1 (Session 1958–9), Q. 299.

scope for moving amendments but to enlarge it'.[1] Be that as it may, there are still occasions when Money Resolutions limit the legislative powers of the House. In 1961, for example, members representing fishing ports in England and Scotland complained that a tightly drawn resolution on the White Fish and Herring Industry Bill meant that 'the committee is absolutely tied. In no way can we seek to amend it.'[2] So, in spite of the contentment of the clerks, it still remains possible for the Executive, via a Money Resolution, to limit the scope for parliamentary lobbying by limiting the range of amendments that may be moved during the legislative process in the House. This is a means by which the Executive may drive the lobbyists out of Westminster and over to Whitehall.

In summary, procedures for the House's control of expenditure, such as the Committee of Supply and Money Resolutions, which were originally designed in the interests of the political process in the House, have been subtly inverted to become techniques for its restraint. And in this the increasingly restrictive interpretation given to Rule 1 has been a factor of major importance. It is the application of that Rule that needs critical appraisal. To dismiss it as being fundamental to the Constitution is to condone all that has been achieved in its name. It will be considered again in Chapter 6, but at this point it will be profitable to examine alternative methods that members have devised for the control of expenditure, viz. House of Commons' control of finance via select committees.

1. Mr D. W. S. Lidderdale, H C 303 (Session 1965–6), p. 12.
2. Mr J. Hoy (Leith), 636 H C Deb., 5s., cc. 1547–63.

4

THE FINANCIAL SELECT COMMITTEES

In the light of the patent inadequacies of the whole House of Commons as a medium for the scrutiny of expenditure proposals, of the realistic conversion of Supply debates into occasions for the discussion of wider policy and even non-financial issues, and of the restrictive effect of Money Resolutions, most hope for parliamentary financial control is staked nowadays on the development of techniques of restraint, check, and enquiry through small select committees. In this respect two committees have won widespread acclaim, viz. the Committee of Public Accounts (established 1861) and the Estimates Committee (first established 1912). There is, however, a third committee—the Select Commitee on Nationalised Industries—which is of more recent origin (1956) and which is acknowledged to have a field of enquiry of increasing financial and economic importance.

The common and fundamental feature in the origins of these committees is that none emerged, spontaneously, on the initiative of the government of the day. They all manifest the collective power of back-benchers in the House of Commons to influence the design of procedural machinery. They are a contradiction of the notion of an Executive dictatorship in Parliament, and they illustrate that the theory of countervailing power is not the monopoly of American capitalism. Whilst the growth of modern democracy in Britain has brought stringent limitations upon the power of elected representatives to interfere directly in the legislative process for granting money, the same representatives, in reaction, have demanded, and secured, the creation of alternative means for financial scrutiny—and now they have three.

Several studies have been made in recent years of these financial committees. Professor Basil Chubb's *The Control of Public Expenditure*, published in 1952, is undoubtedly the most penetrating. He saw the House of Commons to be interested in finance at two distinct levels—'first with questions of policy—what shall be the amount of taxation and expenditure and to what objects public money shall be applied', and, secondly, to 'assure itself that its orders and wishes are carried out by the administration precisely and economically'.[1] He focussed his interest exclusively on the second level and ignored the first. (The first level has been examined above.) But when Chubb wrote, the Select Committee on Nationalised Industries was in embryo and, except for brief mention, it could not be fitted into his general plan. It is the same with K. C. Wheare's *Government by Committee*, published in 1955. It covers a wide selection of parliamentary and executive committees, and the financial committees are studied in the context of a chapter entitled 'Committees to Scrutinise and Control', but as the Select Committee on Nationalised Industries had barely started its life at that time it is briefly treated.[2] More recently, Paul Einzig's *The Control of the Purse* (1959) summarised the evolution and purposes of all three committees in separate but short chapters;[3] and in 1964 the work of the Nationalised Industries Committee was examined briefly in Bernard Crick's *The Reform of Parliament*. He advanced it as the prototype of the kind of 'specialised' committees he wished to see multiplied at Westminster.[4]

Of the three committees the Public Accounts Committee is by

1. Chubb, *op. cit.*, pp. 1–2.
2. K. C. Wheare, *Government by Committee* (OUP, 1955), Ch. VIII.
3. Einzig, *op. cit.*, Chs. 27, 30, 38.
4. Bernard Crick, *The Reform of Parliament* (Weidenfeld and Nicolson, 1964), Ch. 4 and Appendix D.

far the oldest. It originated in 1861 at a time when economy in public expenditure was the avowed aspiration of almost every politician. 'It was no accident in history', wrote a student of public finance recently, 'that Gladstonian traditions of economy in government flourished at a time when voting power was restricted to those with property.'[1] Perhaps there is no certainty in apportioning motives to the financial-administrative changes of the 1860's, but we do know that they were designed to achieve probity and restraint in the handling of public monies at a time when there was widespread apprehension as to the ultimate influence upon government of the impending reform of the franchise. The committee, however, was not wholly Gladstone's doing; it was a replica of Public Accounts Committees operating in Canada from the 1830's, and, as Chubb concluded, it was 'first and generally the work of busy and able parliamentarians who had been interested in procedural problems since the 1820's'.[2]

It was five years after the committee's creation that Gladstone initiated his comprehensive audit reforms in the shape of the Exchequer and Audit Department Act 1866; and it was only then that he could place the Public Accounts Committee in a wider financial context with his well-known explanation that 'the last portion of the circle [that is, the circle of financial control] remained incomplete until the Committee of Public Accounts had done its duty'. Gladstone asserted that it was not till departmental spending had been checked against parliamentary appropriation 'that it could fairly be said that the office of the House, as the real authoritative steward of public moneys, had been discharged'.[3] The metaphorical control circle can still be drawn, and the Public Accounts Committee's enquiry remains essential to it, but in the last half-century the circle has been stretched more and more to embrace the accounts for a greatly expanded area of public activity. Its outline has become vague and its controlling capacity tenuous.

1. A. T. Peacock and D. J. Robertson, *Public Expenditure—Appraisal and Control* (Oliver and Boyd, 1963), p. 4.
2. Chubb, *op. cit.*, p. 33.   3. CLXXXI HC Deb., 3s., c. 1373.

And since the financial arrangements for the vast nationalised industries have, in the main, been placed outside its circumference, Gladstone's method of control is no longer comprehensive, even in its logic.

The second financial committee—the Estimates Committee—originated in more militant circumstances in 1912. It was devised to reinforce Gladstone's control circle at a time when parliamentary scrutiny of expenditure Estimates was patently inadequate. There had been repeated requests from MP's for a new financial committee in the preceding thirty years, more particularly after A. J. Balfour initiated his reforms to Supply procedure in 1896. In response, in 1902, a Select Committee on National Expenditure was appointed and directed 'to enquire whether any plan can be advantageously adopted for enabling the House, by Select Committee or otherwise, more effectively to make an examination, not involving criticism of policy, into the details of National Expenditure'. Although that Committee reported, after much disputation, in favour of a select committee to examine expenditure, governments were not persuaded.[1] Only the relatively aggressive action of back-benchers in 1911–12 finally swayed the issue.

A 'memorandum' with 244 names appended, representing 'the opinion of a very considerable body of members of all parties', and claiming 'the House had not the control over expenditure it was wont to have', was sent to 'every unofficial member of the Conservative, Labour and Liberal parties'. Lloyd George acknowledged this as 'one of the most influentially signed memorials ever presented to a head of government'. It was placed before the Prime Minister with the backing of a 'non-party' deputation, and it was not surprising that in February 1912 Asquith should accept its claims for a new financial committee. It is significant that, in yielding, Asquith stipulated several precautionary conditions, viz. that:

(i) Considerations of questions of policy must be excluded from the purview of the committee.

1. See HC 387 (Session 1902) and HC 343 (Session 1903).

(ii) The control of the House of Commons over Estimates must be strictly unimpaired.

(iii) Treasury control must not be interfered with.

(iv) Ministerial responsibility must in no way be diminished.[1]

In spite of these restraints the Estimates Committee survived. Its existence, however, was sporadic as it was replaced during the war years by Select Committees on National Expenditure. But since 1946, with terms of reference a little less rigid than Asquith's, it has built up an increasingly favourable reputation for constructive work. Indeed, it has kept the Gladstonian control circle from utter disintegration.

The House's third financial select committee entered the parliamentary scene some forty years after the Estimates Committee. Pressures for it were manifest during the 1945–51 Labour Government as a result of limitations placed upon members in questioning Ministers about the newly created nationalised industries, and from the obvious inadequacies of the existing financial committees to scrutinise their vast, and in many ways unique, accounting arrangements.

In 1949 Conservative MP Hugh Molson wrote his now famous article for *The Times*—'Nationalised Industries—Select Committee to secure Parliamentary Control'—pointing out that 'Parliament is . . . faced with a new problem: how to control the strategy of nationalised industries and apply a periodical efficiency check without going as far as that detailed interference which would cause a paralysing centralisation'. Molson recommended a select committee of the House 'served by appropriate staff' to report and 'focus attention upon the most important issues'. This he claimed would make it possible for the House 'to discuss with knowledge and relevance at reasonable intervals the state of each nationalised industry and its proper relation to the national economy as a whole'.[2] And in 1950–1 Professor Laski advocated the establishment

1. *The Times* (London), 13, 17, and 18 February 1912.
2. *The Times* (London), 8 September 1949. Reprinted in A. H. Hanson (Ed.), *Nationalization: A Book of Readings* (Allen and Unwin, 1963), pp. 311–16.

G

of 'a series of Standing Committees in the House of Commons, one for each of the industries concerned . . . [with] power to summon the Minister before it, and also the Chairman of the National Board . . .'[1]

In December 1951, after the change of government, and with Conservative Ministers claiming the protection from parliamentary questions that their predecessors in office had enjoyed, Molson and his followers 'joined by many more Labour MP's,' succeeded in having a select committee established for a preliminary enquiry.[2] The committee was reappointed in December 1952, and it reported in 1953 in favour of the creation, by Standing Order, of a permanent Select Committee on Nationalised Industries.[3]

The recommended committee was not set up until 1955, and, like the Estimates Committee at its birth, it was cribbed with terms of reference that gave little freedom for development. It was appointed to examine the 'Reports and Accounts' and obtain information on 'Current policies and practices' of nationalised industries. There were, however, categorical proscriptions that removed from its jurisdiction matters which:

(a) have been decided by or clearly engage the responsibility of any Ministers;

(b) concern wages and conditions of employment and other questions normally decided by collective bargaining arrangements;

(c) fall to be considered through formal machinery established by the relevant Statutes, or

(d) are matters of day-to-day administration.[4]

This ludicrous and empty brief provoked further back-bench dissatisfactions and the committee reported in November 1955 that it had 'insufficient scope to make enquiries or to obtain further information . . . which would be of any real use to the House'.[5] In

1. H. J. Laski, *Reflections on the Constitution* (Manchester University Press, 1951), p. 91.

2. Bernard Crick, *op. cit.*, p. 90.   3. HC 235 (Session 1952–3).
4. 543 HC Deb., 5s., c. 1470.   5. HC 120 (Session 1955–6), p. v.

1956, after Conservative back-benchers had pressed their dissatisfaction in their party's 1922 Committee, the select committee was re-established, not by Standing Order, but by a resolution of the House giving a welcome liberalisation in its formal scope for action, which it still enjoys.

It is probably more than coincidental that all three of these committees, as well as illustrating the power of Commons back-benchers in procedural issues, were born in political climates that followed important and historic clashes between the House of Lords and the House of Commons in the emergence of Britain's democratic state. The committees may be seen to be the consequence of elected member reaction to the limitations imposed upon the powers of the hereditary chamber. In other words they are manifestations of member-conservatism in the face of a changing balance of power in government. In this respect the Public Accounts Committee was created within twelve months of the Lords rejection of the Paper Duties Repeal Bill in 1860, and the subsequent Commons declaration *inter alia* that 'The rights of granting aids and supplies to the Crown is the Commons' alone'. It followed also the Commons manœuvre whereby the measure for the repeal of the paper duties was ultimately made part of an omnibus taxing bill— the genesis of the present annual and comprehensive Finance Bill— as a result of which the Lords were seen to 'lose even the power of throwing out a money-bill, or would be able to assert it only at the risk of interrupting all legislation affecting the public revenue and expenditure'.[1]

The first Estimates Committee emerged in 1912 in the wake of the Lords' rejection of the budget of 1909 and soon after the first Parliament Act (1911) had reached the statute book. That Act, amongst other things, intensified apprehensions about the growing power of the Executive in Parliament. The committee, and the widespread private member insistence on its creation, can be interpreted as the counterpoise to those developments.

1. T. P. Taswell-Langmead, *English Constitutional History* (Sweet and Maxwell, tenth edition, 1946), p. 618 fn.

And finally, Hugh Molson's article on the nationalised industries was published when the bill for extending nationalisation policy to the steel industry was in its final and troubled stages in the House of Lords; and at the time when the bill to amend the Parliament Act, further reducing the Lords' delaying powers in legislation, was, after a long process, about to receive the Royal Assent. It was a time, too, when there was an air of disquiet about growing Executive power; and when complaints about bureaucratic habits had profound electoral significance.

It is conjectural, but highly probable, that the landmarks over the last century in the decline of the powers of the House of Lords have also been the high-water marks of representatives' reaction in the defence of the House of Commons against Executive encroachments.

Formal provisions

Like their titles, the official terms of reference of the three committees (as they stand in 1965) give a general indication of their relative financial interests:

The Committee of Public Accounts is authorised by Standing Order (at present No. 79) to examine:

. . . accounts showing the appropriation of the sums granted by Parliament to meet the public expenditure, and of such other accounts laid before Parliament as the committee may think fit . . .

The Estimates Committee has power under Standing Order (at present No. 80) to:

. . . examine such of the estimates presented to this House as may seem fit to the committee and report how, if at all, the policy implied in those estimates may be carried out more economically and, if the committee think fit, to consider the principal variations between the estimates and those relating to the previous financial year and the form in which the Estimates are presented to the House, . . .

And the Select Committee on Nationalised Industries is authorised, each session, to:

. . . examine the Reports and Accounts of the Nationalised Industries established by Statute, whose controlling Boards are wholly appointed by Ministers of the Crown and whose annual receipts are not wholly or mainly derived from moneys provided by Parliament or advanced from the Exchequer.

Two of the committees—Public Accounts and Nationalised Industries—are formally restricted to working within the wake of policy performed. The former has an arid-looking accounting brief, to examine financial statistics at the end of each annual accounting period; and the latter is empowered to look beyond prosaic accounting detail and into the wider interests of the reports of nationalised industries, which, generally speaking, relate to policies decided and executed rather than policies being conceived. The Estimates Committee, on the other hand, is authorised to look at current expenditure plans—not accounts. In theory it lives in the present financial world, and possibly the next, as distinct from the last; it examines selected subjects from the Executive's annual and supplementary estimates of expenditure, all of which are the quantitative expression of current policy; and, expressing characteristic Executive caution, it is formally limited to reporting 'how, if at all, the policy implied in those estimates may be carried out more economically . . .' But things are seldom what they seem. It will be shown that all three committees, in reality, have significance and functions substantially different from those formally allotted to them.

Two of the committees have their terms of reference expressed with relative permanence in the Standing Orders of the House. This recognition was given the Committee of Public Accounts before its first anniversary, in 1862. But the Estimates Committee had to wait half a century (until 1961) for the same accolade. The Select Committee on Nationalised Industries, although its chairman in 1962 claimed the 'parliamentary experiment' had 'worked', is still apparently serving its apprenticeship[1]; it awaits a formal declaration of its belonging, and, until then, it has to be re-established, by resolution, each session. The House hastens slowly when it comes to declaring a permanent place in its Standing Orders for select committees of enquiry.

The House, however, has not been averse to making changes in committee sizes, and, curiously, changes have always been to enlarge the membership, never to reduce it. Although a Standing Order (at present No. 69) provides that 'No select committee shall, without leave of the House, consist of more than fifteen members . . .' there are variations. The Committee of Public Accounts was originally nine in number; then in 1870 it was increased to eleven; and finally to fifteen in 1893. That fifteen includes the Financial Secretary to the Treasury, who seldom attends, so the effective number is fourteen. The Estimates Committee began in 1912 at fifteen strong, but as a result of pressure, either from the committee itself or from back-benchers in the House, it became twenty-four strong in 1921, twenty-eight in 1924, thirty-six in 1948, and in July 1960 it was enlarged to its existing forty-three members. The Select Committee on Nationalised Industries has not yet been altered from its original thirteen members.

Set up at the beginning of every session, the three committees, collectively, provide places for up to seventy members to engage in detailed enquiry into matters of social importance. Except for one ministerial representative on the Public Accounts Committee they are usually comprised of back-benchers, with the political parties being represented roughly in proportion to their representation in the House. Without official appointments to absorb their experienced members, the Opposition party is normally in a position to nominate members with a wider knowledge and experience of public administration than is the case for the government side. The committees appoint their own chairmen but, obviously, the party

1. Sir Toby Low, 'The Select Committee on Nationalised Industries', *Public Administration*, vol 40 (Spring, 1962), pp. 1–15. Reprinted in Hanson, *op. cit.*, pp. 322–38.

Whips have a say in this. The Committee of Public Accounts is the sole example where the chairman is chosen from its Opposition members. This practice, not normally provided for, has been followed since 1870. It is said to prevail because 'as the [Committee] is looking at what is past, the government is prepared to tolerate the choice of a chairman who will not be disposed to see mistakes glossed over or whitewashed'.[1] The Select Committee on Estimates, which alone of the three committees works by delegating its enquiry functions to sub-committees, appoints its chairman from the government party members; it is customary, however, for Opposition members to be appointed to the chairs of some of the sub-committees. The Chairman of the Select Committee on Nationalised Industries has, to date, been a government supporter.

The Public Accounts Committee produces one main report each session, the product of thirty to forty hearings and the examination of as many officials through about 4,000 questions. The Estimates Committee works through its half-dozen sub-committees and may produce a dozen or more reports a session, usually on specific topics of enquiry (e.g. Treasury Control, the War Office, Variations in Estimates, Supplementary Estimates, London's Airports, the Ministry of Agriculture, Fisheries and Food). And with the enquiries into nationalised industries the practice, so far, has been to examine the accounts and reports of one industry (gas, railways, coal, British Overseas Airways Corporation, etc.) per session; it works over thirty to forty sittings, calling witnesses from the appropriate public industry and the relevant departments.

The reports of all three of the committees are published in the House of Commons series of papers on the order of the House. All the reports presume that answers or comments will be made by the appropriate department, or public industry, via the responsible Minister. It is the practice for the ministerial responses, and the committee's further remarks, to be published as a 'Special Report' in the case of the Estimates and Nationalised Industries Committees, or with the principal report of the following session in the case of

1. K. C. Wheare, *Government by Committee*, *op. cit.*, p. 211.

the Committee of Public Accounts. And debates in the House are
now held, each session, on some aspects of selected reports.

Membership

Although it has been claimed that committees like these provide
'the only truly valuable form of service still open to the private
member',[1] there is no clear criterion for member selection. Selection
is essentially a party matter left to Whip-member-party negotiations.
Most committee members, particularly the chairmen, enjoy com-
fortable majorities in their electorates and have relative security in
giving the committee the time and attention it demands. A Conservative member of the Estimates Committee (Captain Litchfield),
himself with a constituency majority of 15,000, once explained to
the House that 'I do not think one gets on it by acclamation or vote
. . . it is partly merit, partly integrity and chiefly luck'.[2]

   The motives that members have in giving their talents and time to
the committees of the House are various and are difficult to define.
For some, there is a personal satisfaction in giving 'service' to the
House and this ought not to be discounted in its importance. For
others, there are political advantages available such as the opportunity for exhibiting one's ability—in examining witnesses or in analysing problems of administration. And each committee provides a
relatively small forum via which a member may become known to
civil servants, to party leaders, and to the limited number of
readers of committee reports, including journalists. For the chairman
of a financial committee there is undoubted social and political
prestige accruing by virtue of being the incumbent of the chair.
The fact of chairmanship usually gains reference in books of bio-
graphical detail. And there is for a chairman the reward of power,
although this is a different power from that a Minister of State
enjoys. It is not a direct power over people, but a power of enquiry
and revelation. Each committee has a role requiring it to appraise
critically governmental or quasi-governmental activity. The chairman's task, therefore, demands more than average political skill. He

   1. Christopher Hollis, *Can Parliament Survive?* (Hollis and Carter, 1949), p. 66.
   2. 669 HC Deb., 5s., c. 1178.

has to reconcile the divergent party-political and personal interests of committee members with the prestige and status of his committee in the House, his own satisfaction, and perhaps his own political ambition. Obviously a great deal transpires within each committee that is not open politics, but it is clear that the relationships between members are different from those evident in the House. Possibly Labour MP Sir George Benson's experiences are indicative of a chairman's lot (Benson was Chairman of the Public Accounts Committee 1952–8). He claimed '. . . on occasions unanimity has been rather difficult to obtain'; and recalled 'one occasion as Chairman when I sat up until after midnight . . . wrestling with two members of the Conservative Party who wanted to slam their own government more severely than I thought necessary'.[1] A successful chairman is a man who can steer his committee (or permit it to be steered) as close to party political shoals as possible, without letting it founder.

Beyond personal satisfaction, the rewards to chairmen for committee achievements are varied. There is no remuneration involved: the tradition of voluntary service dies hard. Sir George Benson's knighthood was undoubtedly a reward for his long period of service to the Public Accounts Committee (1929–31 and from 1935–59). However, Mr Harold Wilson's reward for service to the same committee (as Chairman 1959–62) was not from the royal sword. He exploited its potential as 'one of the few ways in which Members of the House of Commons can acquire a detailed insight into the problems of Departmental administration and management'.[2] The Chair afforded him, as an Opposition member, unequalled access to official information, and he had the capacity to use the advantage well. As an ex-bureaucrat, and with ministerial experience, he was a formidable scourge of official witnesses. One of his colleagues saw him as 'a very nice person who has, inside a velvet glove, the toughest and hardest of fists'.[3] Wilson, himself, has spoken of the committee as 'the only blood sport which is sanctioned by Parlia-

1. 668 HC Deb., 5s., c. 1573.   2. Mr A. Barber, 668 HC Deb., 5s., c. 1580.
3. Mr G. Chetwynd, 650 HC Deb., 5s., c. 667.

ment and which is enjoined upon . . . hon. Members as a parliamentary duty'.[1] There is no doubt that civil servant Sir Thomas
Padmore (as Second Secretary, Treasury) will long remember his
verbal skirmish with Wilson when seeking from the committee
permanent authority for the Executive to vary, without prior
parliamentary approval, grants made for subscriptions to international organisations.[2] And Wilson's notoriety as chairman was
not only in the minds of civil servants. He turned it to wider
advantage precisely on the day of the press announcement of his
decision 'to stand against Mr Gaitskell for the Leadership of the
Labour Party'. On Friday, 21 October 1960, the *Guardian* published
his lengthy article on 'The Control of Public Expenditure' which
emphasised, prophetically, the troubles facing the committee and
the Parliament, in financing and controlling scientific research and
development. This was Wilson-type publicity; if it did not win
him the leadership in 1960 it was not to his disadvantage in February
1963. And his successor to the chair, Labour M P Douglas Houghton,
signed a report that followed up the attacks that Wilson's committee made on 'open-ended' research contracts. In doing this
Houghton could rely upon Wilson (by then Leader of the Opposition) to back him in the House. It is significant that upon the change
of government in 1964 Houghton received immediate appointment
to Wilson's cabinet.

There is a similar inconsistency in the careers of the Conservative
Party chairmen of the Public Accounts Committee. Two of the
four chairmen between 1945 and 1951, Mr Osbert Peake and Mr
Ralph Assheton, went to the House of Lords. The former found the
committee a stepping stone to the Ministry (in 1951) and to
cabinet rank (1954); and it led the latter to the Chair of the Select
Committee on Nationalised Industries. The other two held the
chair during the uncertain period 1950–1—the first, the Rt Hon
Sir Ronald Cross, became Governor of Tasmania (1951–8), and the
second, Captain Charles Waterhouse, became Chairman of the

1. *ibid.* c. 641.
2. H C 251–1 (Session 1961–2), QQ. 2613–32.

Estimates Committee from 1953 until the Suez crisis affected his career in 1957. Upon the return of the Conservatives to Opposition in 1964 an ex-Financial Secretary to the Treasury (Mr Boyd-Carpenter) took on the responsibilities of Committee of Public Accounts leadership.

From the post-war record of the Estimates Committee, on the other hand, it looks that its chairmen (all Conservative or Labour Party members) cannot expect illustrious career prospects. Theirs is a difficult task. The sub-committees often penetrate fields of current policy—much to the embarrassment of the Executive—and it is the chairman of the full committee who takes the kicks. It is significant that most of the post-war chairmen of the Estimates Committee have assumed their responsibilities towards the end of their political careers.[1]

But in the case of the chairmen of the Select Committee on the Nationalised Industries, who until 1964 were all Conservative Party men, there has been one consistent career prospect—elevation to the peerage. The committee's first protagonist—Mr Hugh Molson—became a life peer; and its first three chairmen, all Oxford graduates, became peers of first creation.[2] (And as only 6 per cent of MP's between 1918 and 1959 received peerages, that looks significant.[3]) However, it cannot be said categorically that the instrument of peerage has helped the Minister to keep the committee within his sphere of influence. Part of the acknowledged success of the committee stems from the pressures it has exerted upon Ministers in the interests of particular industries. It is probable that the prospects of peerage have provided able and altruistic Conservative Party chairmen capable of fulfilling an otherwise thankless task.

A common feature of these committees is the non-party approach that prevails in their labours. It seems that a prerequisite of success

1. 1945–50 B. Kirby; 1950–1 A. Anderson; 1951–3 Sir R. Glyn; 1953–7 Colonel C. Waterhouse; 1957–61 R. Turton; 1961–4 Sir G. Nicholson; 1964 W. Hamilton.

2. 1951–4 Ralph Assheton; 1954–6 Sir Patrick Spens; 1957–61 Sir Toby Low; 1961–4 Sir Richard Nugent; 1965 E. Popplewell.

3. Philip W. Buck, *Amateurs and Professionals in British Politics, 1918–1959* (University of Chicago Press, 1963), p. 42.

for a committee chairman is a capacity to subordinate the tempta-
tions to engage in party politics to a notion for rectitude in public
affairs. Harold Wilson, as Chairman of the Public Accounts
Committee, once said that that committee was 'not a battle ground
of party faction . . . in the 100 years of its existence there are only
sixty-four recorded divisions';[1] and when speaking in the House on
his Committee's report he saw himself 'not speaking for the official
Opposition' but as the committee's chairman.[2] Sir Godfrey Nicholson, Chairman of the Estimates Committee 1961–4, said: 'I see no
objection at all to the findings of the Public Accounts Committee and
the Estimates Committee being used as weapons of party warfare
across the floor of the House. Where I feel party political argument
is completely inapposite is in the actual work of the Committee'.[3]
And Hugh Molson's expectation for a Select Committee of Nationalised Industries was that '. . . in the seclusion of a committee room
there may be comparative freedom from political prejudice'.[4] This,
apparently, was realised. By 1961 the retiring-chairman of that
committee (Sir Toby Low) could report 'party political controversy
has been absent. . . .' There had, he said, been 'only one division'.[5]

Basically, these three committees owe their origins and their
continued existence to the efforts of a nucleus of ardent back-
benchers who seek to make a more direct contribution to the process
of government than is possible from the floor of the House. There
is an element of service motivating members in their committee
work, and an expectation that in the relative quiet of a committee
room, removed from publicity, they can be non-party political
beings for a few hours each week. Indeed, it is the relative freedom
from party restraint afforded by these committees that makes the
front-benchers, on both sides, suspicious of their potential.

Committee reports

The clear logic of each committee's activities is that it will report
back to the House for the information of the general body of

1. 650 HC Deb., 5s., c. 643.   2. *ibid*, c. 637.   3. *ibid*, c. 655.
4. HC 235 (Session 1952–3), Q. 317.   5. Hanson, *op. cit.*, p. 336.

members. It has always been a matter of dispute as to what subsequent action the House should take—whether the members should consider reports merely as information available to them; or whether formal provision should be made for debates specifically on them. There were attempts to start annual debates on reports of the Committee of Public Accounts as early as 1905; but support was lacking and the practice did not survive the First World War. Since 1934 there has been a formal provision in the Standing Order providing for 'Business of Supply' (S.O. No. 18) that reports of the Public Accounts and Estimates Committees are eligible to be debated on an 'allotted' Supply day. But until 1960 this was seldom used. Chubb suggested that 'Important as is much contained in the reports, it is only when they mention a subject of particular current interest, of a scandalous nature or with political repercussions, that the House finds them interesting enough to give time for discussion'.[1] K. C. Wheare, on the other hand, saw restraint in the minds of committee members: 'The chairmen of these committees, generally speaking, feel that they ought not to put down motions drawing attention to the report of their committee, and that this self-denying ordinance extends to the members of the committee also. Some of them feel diffidence even in joining in a debate which has been initiated by other private members'.[2] And a Clerk of the House (Sir Edward Fellowes) could not see the debates on the reports of the Estimates Committee being successful for 'they are forbidden to deal with policy'. They are concerned, he said, only in details 'which is not what interests the House'.[3]

The issue, however, is more difficult than the commentators acknowledge. The chairman, in each case, is consistently concerned with his committee's reputation in the eyes of the Executive, the House and the senior officials. He fears that incisive debate in the open parliamentary forum, under the full glare of press publicity, will undermine rather than strengthen the effectiveness of his committee as a medium of enquiry. Parliamentary committees of

1. Chubb, *op. cit.*, p. 193.   2. Wheare, *op. cit.*, p. 232.
3. HC 92–1 (Session 1958–9), QQ. 285–9.

enquiry depend as much upon human co-operation as they do upon their formal powers of sanction. There is a constant fear that in the heat of political conflict the flow of official information might evaporate. A committee chairman seldom cherishes the sight of a hard-won report suffering the vagaries of political conflict in the House. Relatively, the chairman's is a long-term interest, whereas the floor of the House is the arena for immediate political gain.

One of the surprising outcomes of the Conservative back-bench dissension (the 'Hinchingbrooke revolt') about the financial arrangements in 1960 was the assurance of the Leader of the House (R. A. Butler) that in future three days per session were to be made available on the floor of the House for debating reports of the financial committees. One day was to be in government time and two in Opposition time (two allotted Supply days).[1] And in the subsequent sessions these opportunities have been used—but not always to the extent of three days. In view of the scepticism about the reform it is interesting to look at the consequences.

Debates in the House on the reports of the financial committees have an obvious educative potential. They provide for an exposition in public of the major findings of a committee, and a forum for back-benchers to follow up unsatisfactory responses on the part of the administration. It is significant that committee chairmen have insisted that ministerial responses must be available before a debate takes place.

The quality of debate, however, has varied. Attendance, generally, has been poor and there have been frequent allegations about lack of interest. Committee members have tended to use the debates as occasions for self-congratulation in recognition of the sacrifices in time and effort made on a committee's behalf. Moreover, there has been an artificial air engendered by disingenuous assertions that the debates should be 'non-political'. This has called for split personalities and some doubletalk, and not all members have been adept at it. Harold Wilson emphasised that at these times 'the confrontation . . . is not between Government and Opposition but

1. 627 H C Deb., 5s., cc. 1292–302.

between the House of Commons . . . and the Government'.[1] And once, when party politics intruded, the Financial Secretary to the Treasury (Mr Anthony Barber) complained that it had not occurred to him that the occasion would be used 'to continue the Opposition's campaign against retired Ministers and retired civil servants taking up jobs in industry and commerce'. 'No mention', he claimed, 'appears in any of the Reports of the Committee . . .' (it was, in fact, a feature of the printed evidence), and no 'notice' had been given him.[2] One could be sympathetic with the government back-bencher who referred to a debate in 1962 as 'the battle of flowers'.[3]

But for the advocates of the practice of debating reports there must be encouragement in the debates on the Estimates Committee's report on the War Office and its further report on the relevant Minister's 'observations';[4] and also in the consequences of the debates on the reports of the Committee of Public Accounts that emphasised the threats to conventional methods of financial control occasioned by the Government's contractual arrangements for guided missiles.[5]

In the case of the Estimates Committee and the War Office, the chairman (Sir Godfrey Nicholson) told the House that 'a Committee of Members . . . came back from its enquiries deeply disturbed',[6] and the Conservative Party chairman of the sub-committee that undertook the investigation (Mr R. Carr) emphasised the dissatisfaction of the sub-committee in 'the manner in which the War Office exercises effective control over the total cost of the Army';[7] and he expressed surprise and concern that 'such a rudimentary system of financial control should have been permitted to last for so long'.[8] In winding up that debate the Chairman of the Estimates Committee referred to its 'useful purpose' in spite of the 'very small attendance', and he added an ominous warning to the Executive—

1. 632 HC Deb., 5s., c. 894.   2. 668 HC Deb., 5s., c. 1591–2.
3. Sir H. d'Avigdor Goldsmid, 669 HC Deb., 5s., c. 1194.
4. *ibid*, 1158–222; and see HC 251–I (Session 1960–1) and HC 183–I (Session 1963–4).
5. HC 256–I (Session 1959–60); 632 HC Deb., 5s., cc. 902–9.
6. 669 HC Deb., 5s., c. 1222.   7. *ibid*, c. 1157.   8. *ibid*, c. 1162.

'now we have the chance of these two debates every year . . . I hope that it will be recognised by all Departments that we mean to follow-up . . . do not let any Government Department, still less the War Office, think that the Estimates Committee will allow the grass to grow under its feet'.[1]

In the case of the reports of the Committee of Public Accounts the debates have been profitable. The committee's report for 1959–60, for example, prepared under the chairmanship of Harold Wilson, asserted that open-ended research contracts were 'something new in the financial history of this country', were 'inevitably' open to abuse; and that 'control in the past was seriously inadequate'. It called for 'new methods of supervision at the highest level'.[2] The debates on this and subsequent reports built up a substantial measure of disquiet, and when it became known, before the general election in 1964, that a contractor had gained a profit of £5·7 millions on research and development costing £7 millions, political fire raged.[3] Wilson, by then Leader of the Opposition, was equipped to argue pungently from a position of informed confidence. The issue gave wide currency to the work of the committee and of the Comptroller and Auditor-General, but when the conflict was at its most vigorous, and acrid, it is significant that the reports of the committee were not formally the subject of debate.[4] Unquestionably the debates held, and the possibility of more, led the Government in 1964 to commission an 'independent investigation into the pricing and contract procedures for guided weapons'.[5] And, ultimately, when 'excessive profits' were revealed, the contractor arranged to repay £4·25 millions to the Exchequer.

The political sanctions latent in the formal provision of Supply-day debates on the reports of the financial committees are salutary. They make it difficult for a government to evade the Opposition's pressure for full-scale polemics on a committee's critical comments.

1. *ibid*, c. 1220.   2. HC 256-1 (Session 1959–60), p. xxxv.
3. HC 183–1 (Session 1963–4).
4. 694 HC Deb., 5s., cc. 408–551; and see 699 HC Deb., 5s., cc. 1801–44.
5. First Report of the Inquiry into the Pricing of Ministry of Aviation Contracts—Cmnd 2428.

But poor attendances at most of the debates indicate that the presumption that they are a logical conclusion to a committee's efforts, regardless of its findings, is misplaced. To make these debates mandatory would impose an unreasonably rigid pattern of behaviour upon the national political forum. There are advantages in leaving them at the discretion of the Opposition.

It is significant, however, that when R. A. Butler announced in 1960 that three days per session were to be used for debating reports of both the Public Accounts Committee and the Estimates Committee he made only passing reference to the reports of the Select Committee on Nationalised Industries.[1] They have subsequently been debated, but never on a Supply day. There is a distinct reticence in the affairs of the House to classify that committee as being 'financial'. Its work is considered to be outside Gladstone's sequence of control and, hence, beyond the financial pale. When contemplating debate on the affairs of a nationalised industry, Prime Minister Sir Anthony Eden once claimed it to be 'doubtful whether Supply days, which have a special connotation, are suitable for [that] kind of discussion'.[2] And Hugh Molson was similarly opposed. He feared it would mean that in the event of a change of government the errors of the board [of a nationalised industry] would be likely to recoil upon the new Opposition' and, as the Opposition chose the topic of debate on a Supply day, he claimed 'there would probably be no debate . . . however great the need to escape blunders and abuses'. He did not acknowledge, however, that this problem applied to many facets of public administration whenever parties changed sides in the House. Molson also claimed, and with some justification, that to debate the reports in the Committee of Supply would reduce the opportunities for debates on departmental administration, and that the debates would suffer the committee's prohibition upon reference to the need for new legislation.[3] But he failed to point out that in the broad spectrum of governmental affairs, the similarity in the objectives of all three financial select

1. 627 HC Deb., 5s., cc. 1292–302.   2. 547 HC Deb., 5s., c. 557.
3. Hanson, *op. cit.*, p. 314.

H

committees is increasingly evident, and that, in consequence, there is
no justification for differential procedures when it comes to debating
their reports in the House. Basically, there is need for a clarification
of purpose and method in the debating of reports, just as there is
(see Chapter 6) in the operation of the committees themselves.

Expert assistance

Much discussion has ensued for and against reinforcing the activities
of the three committees with expert assistance. In this regard it is
generally held that the Public Accounts Committee is well served.
'Professional strength is added to its work', said its chairman
recently, 'by the inestimable services of the Comptroller and
Auditor-General.'[1] And, it is worth noting, the Comptroller has a
staff of approximately 600 audit officials, working mostly out in the
departments, who contribute to the annual report he presents to the
House. The other financial committees have nothing like that
intelligence force to help their equally complex enquiries.

The Comptroller and Auditor-General explained his relationships
with the Public Accounts Committee as being 'complementary'.
He said he had no real power other than reporting to Parliament.
He could not, for instance, 'impose any disallowances' or 'insist on
Departments complying with his views'. The effectiveness of the
whole system, he asserted, really depended on 'the standing and
reputation' of the Committee of Public Accounts.[2] But undoubtedly, the reverse is equally true—the committee depends upon the
Comptroller. Sir Edward (later Lord) Bridges once explained their
relationship as: the Comptroller 'puts up a lot of game for the
Committee to have a shot at'.[3] At every meeting, before the shoot-
ing, the Comptroller consults the committee's chairman and its
clerk; they all 'consider the agenda' and discuss 'matters arising out
of the report in order that the chairman may be better able to
conduct the examination of the witnesses in such a way to bring out

1. Harold Wilson, 'The Control of Public Expenditure', the *Guardian*, 21 October
1960.
2. Sir Frank Tribe, *The Table*, vol XXVI (1957), pp. 34–9.
3. HC 235 (Session 1952–3), Q. 884.

all the essential facts'. The Comptroller claims that he is treated as 'an Officer of the House of Commons' and is given their 'rights and privileges';[1] in fact, he prepares the committee's draft report.

It is understandable, therefore, that there are advocates for making similar professional assistance available to the other committees. On the establishment of the Estimates Committee in 1912 a member of the House (Colonel R. Williams) asserted that if the Committee 'was to do anything at all, it must have an officer of the House similar to the Comptroller and Auditor-General . . . to guide them'. Otherwise, he warned, 'they would really be groping in the dark'.[2] And in 1918 the Select Committee on National Expenditure, after an enquiry into Supply procedure, recommended, but in vain, the establishment of an office of 'Examiner of the Estimates' to assist the committee.[3] Then in 1926 the Estimates Committee recommended its own increase in size, from twenty-four to twenty-eight, so that it could function through sub-committees to which it could co-opt 'experts'; but the Government did no more than place an official of the Treasury at its disposal.[4] In 1931 a Select Committee on Procedure was urged 'very strongly' that a 'technical adviser' should be attached to the committee because 'Estimates are very technical things, and it needs an expert to understand them'. The Rt Hon Sir Herbert Samuel claimed that members were 'helpless' in the face of great blocks of Estimates that are circulated each year.[5] The subject received yet another airing before the Select Committee on Procedure in 1945–6, when Mr Osbert Peake, Chairman of the Public Accounts Committee and ex-member of the Estimates Committee, alleged that the latter 'must have expert guidance if they are going to be effective'. Peake wanted to have '. . . somebody who is not a servant of the Executive to guide them in their labours. . . .'[6] In 1951 Laski contended that 'To make the Estimates

---

1. Sir Frank Tribe, op. cit.   2. The Times (London), 18 April 1912.
3. HC 121 (Session 1918).
4. See K. C. Wheare, Government by Committee, op. cit., pp. 222–3.
5. HC 161 (Session 1930–1), Q. 2356.
6. HC 189–1 (Session 1945–6), Qs. 3979–81. Quoted in full in K. C. Wheare, Government by Committee, op. cit., p. 224.

Committee a really successful instrument of control, it would need, first of all, an official with a status like that of the Comptroller and Auditor-General, with a staff at his disposal with experience of the Treasury. . . .'[1] And in 1965 the Estimates Committee, via a Special Report, asked to be given authority '. . . to engage the services of someone with technical or scientific knowledge on an *ad hoc* basis for the purpose of a particular enquiry or part of an enquiry, either to supply information which was not readily available or to elucidate matters of complexity . . .'[2]

The unprecedented expansion in governmental expenditure in recent years, its extensive social and economic ramifications, and the increasing volume and apparent complexity of the associated documents, have given the claims for professional assistance for the Estimates Committee seemingly wider importance. There looks now to be an unanswerable case. In 1950, for example, the Crick Committee on 'The Form of Government Accounts' asserted 'that the Estimates are so clogged with details about salaries that they fail, by their sheer bulk, to give a clear picture of the Departments' projected outlay'.[3] And, more recently, the Treasury in pressing for reform claimed 'that the sheer bulk and complexity of the present documents is a formidable obstacle to understanding at all levels'.[4] There was also cause for concern when the Chairman of the Estimates Committee declared in 1961 that 'after many years in Parliament [in fact, twenty-four years] I have never understood the first thing about Supplementary Estimates. It is a terrible confession, but I think it goes for many members of Parliament, if not most.'[5] There have been some important reforms to the expenditure documents since 1962, particularly the addition of details to show the formal relationship between the major totals of estimated expenditure and the relevant categories in the national (social) accounts. The reforms, however, have been restricted by the need to preserve the principles of strictly annual cash accounting and

1. Laski, *Reflections on the Constitution, op. cit.*, p. 40.
2. HC 161 (Session 1964–5), p. 3.   3. Cmd 7969, p. 42.
4. HC 184 (Session 1960–1), p. 1.
5. Sir Godfrey Nicholson, 652 HC Deb., 5s., c. 329.

departmental accountability; the main objective in the recent changes was to achieve simplification by reducing the main Estimates document to a volume of 450 pages comprising 1,350 sub-heads of expenditure. Bulk, it appears, is inevitable; statistics of cash allocations abound, and prose is secondary. So far as the Estimates Committee is concerned, there is an assumption that forty-three members acting collectively, or through sub-committees, will be more capable of analysing and understanding expenditure documents, than members acting singly; and that expert assistance is not required.

Furthermore, the committee has the problem of counteracting evasive manœuvres on the part of the Executive. There was, for example, considerable feeling in the *cri de cœur* of a member of the Estimates Committee in 1962 'that the moment it is announced that the Select Committee . . . intends to investigate a given subject the Ministry concerned promptly makes it known that it is setting up a working committee . . . to flummox and bewilder the Select Committee'.[1] On the face of the existing committee-Executive relationships, an expert secretariat for the committee would appear to be a rational means of overcoming the obvious disadvantages it faces.

There is much the same story, although over a shorter period, with the Select Committee on Nationalised Industries. In 1950 Laski advocated for the envisaged committee 'a small but highly expert secretariat';[2] and after preliminary enquiries into the feasibility of a regular committee in this sphere, an exploratory select committee in 1952 proposed that the final body should have the assistance of 'a permanent official of a status roughly equivalent to that of the Comptroller and Auditor-General' who would work 'with the assistance of at least one professional accountant . . . in order to direct the committee's attention to matters requiring examination'.[3] But from the first the Government made its opposition to such a development perfectly clear. And when the committee

1. Sir F. Markham, 652 HC Deb., 5s., c. 329.
2. Laski, *Reflections on the Constitution*, op. cit., p. 91.
3. HC 235 (Session 1952–3), p. xii.

was launched in 1956 it had the assistance only of a clerk and a Treasury adviser. In 1959, however, after the benefit of three sessions' experience, the committee reported against having an official with the status of the Comptroller and Auditor-General. It suggested two ways in which assistance from specialists would be beneficial. 'First, an accountant with experience of industrial and commercial accounts would have been very helpful in analysing the formidable tables of figures. . . . Secondly, a research worker with training in economics could have informed your Committee about what had been written on the subject.' 'With this kind of help', the committee concluded, 'enquiries might have been shorter and more effective' and 'it is possible that at least one additional enquiry might have been completed in the same period'.[1]

During its enquiry in 1959 the Select Committee on Nationalised Industries summoned the Leader of the House (R. A. Butler) to give evidence. He countered their pressures for expert assistance by suggesting the positive contribution that a Treasury official could make to their enquiries. But this met an unqualified negative—'anyone from the Executive, any man from the Treasury . . . would not meet our requirements', rejoined the chairman. Then the committee tested on the Minister the idea that a firm of chartered accountants be appointed to 'take the reports and accounts and . . . interpret them to us'. As the chairman put it, 'I want to have someone whom I could talk to and get him to interpret accounts rightly to me. . . . One has that kind of person to help . . . if one is concerned with business.' But the Minister was not moved. He explained, he was 'not awfully keen about bringing in what amounts to a commercial firm into . . . transactions with Parliament and with the Nationalised Industries', and warned 'we are on the edge of an innovation here which we want to watch very carefully before we actually undertake it'.[2]

The pressures of 1959 were, however, not without effect. Subsequently the Minister offered the committee a compromise: the appointment of an 'Assessor' to be paid a fee 'according to the

1. H C 276 (Session 1958–9), p. **iv**.   2. *ibid*, QQ. 243, 254, 263, 267.

amount of work he actually did', and for whose choice the Minister proposed: 'You could no doubt obtain advice from the Clerk of the House and from Whitehall'. In this respect much transpired that was not revealed. The committee (in its report) ambiguously left it to 'the House' to decide 'whether the power should be given to any future Select Committee on Nationalised Industries to appoint an assessor'.[1] No decision, it seems, has yet been taken, even though, in his valedictory review of the committee's work, the chairman of 1959 (Sir Toby Low) recorded: 'I did myself at one time feel the lack of a professional accountant at my elbow', and 'the other need I felt from time to time was for a trained economist to put my nose on the right scent so that the Committee would not waste their time running along false trails'.[2]

Responsible government in Britain is based on the theory of lay control of experts, but with the expansion of the functions of the State, both in their scope and complexity, the lay element frequently asserts, often legitimately, that the gap between theory and practice is vast. This is the very problem facing the Estimates and Nationalised Industries Committees in the performance of their control functions. Their quest for an intelligence staff to sift and classify the multifarious expenditure details of every service of State (departmental or corporative) so as to facilitate their interpretations, looks in every respect to be logical and necessary. And on an analogy with the Comptroller and Auditor-General, who once said, 'My job is to ascertain the facts. It is for the Public Accounts Committee to form a judgement on them',[3] the case is convincing. But what case can be made against such an assessment?

For the nationalised industries the continuing problem is how much parliamentary interference is compatible with the theory of their corporate independence. The proposal for a 'new kind of Comptroller and Auditor-General' for this sphere was finally dismissed by the committee on grounds that it '. . . would most

1. *ibid*, Appendix, p. 49, and p. ix.
2. *Public Administration* (Spring, 1962), vol 40, p. 7.
3. HC 228 (Session 1961–2), Q. 265.

probably lead, or would appear to be leading, towards a Grand Inquisition into the nationalised industries by officials acting on behalf of Parliament'.[1] Whilst this kind of interference might be acceptable for ministerial departments in the name of Gladstonian rectitude in the use of public moneys, it is not necessarily appropriate to the State's industrial activities. Indeed, the Comptroller and Auditor-General now admits of an intrusion into departmental affairs much deeper than was the case twenty years ago; nowadays, he claims '. . . public spending is scrutinised for instances of waste, inefficiency or weakness of system'.[2] But as agreeable as these objectives are, a quest for them, through parliamentary enquiry into the nationalised industries, must prompt the question 'What does corporate independence really mean?' And that requires an answer before the question of expert assistance can be reasoned out.

Is it the same with the Estimates Committee? Is there any validity in the case for an 'Examiner of Estimates' or, as Henry Higgs once claimed, an 'Inspector-General of Finance' as adviser to the committee?[3] In the absence of an official declaration of purpose it is understandable that many people still harbour the view that the committee's function is to fulfil comprehensive and detailed scrutiny of every detail of every expenditure proposal. But, as in the Committee of Supply, this has long been rejected even as an aspiration. Since 1946 the committee, by functioning through its sub-committees, has given specific attention only to seven or eight subjects of expenditure annually, plus its scrutiny of Supplementary Estimates and Variations in Estimates. Comprehensive scrutiny of the Estimates—except, perhaps, some Supplementary Estimates—is not attempted. The committee acts on the assumption that the latent threat of scrutiny will, in most cases, impose sufficient restraint upon official excesses, inefficiency and wastefulness. Does it still need help?

If the estimates are seen to be the Executive's requests for cash grants to meet its annual expenditure needs then the problem is not

1. HC 276 (Session 1958–9), p. vi.

2. Sir Edmund Compton, *Control of Public Expenditure* (Address to the Institute of Municipal Treasurers and Accountants, 1960), p. 16.

3. Henry Higgs, *Financial Reform* (Macmillan, 1924), pp. 37, 62–4.

so much their complexity as their comprehensiveness. They are, in that respect, statistical tables of expenditure; and the function of the Estimates Committee is to seek the elaboration of particular totals in terms of the efficient use of available resources. And for such a task the committee is free to call witnesses—official and non-official —and to request, and possibly insist upon, explanations via written submissions and oral evidence. The committee's need in this is not necessarily for a person analogous to an audit adviser, or for an accountant, or—as it functions at present—for an economist. It needs a large supply of common sense and enquiring zeal.

But if the Estimates are seen as the fiscal expression of a large part of the expenditure policies within the public sector of the economy, and which, individually and collectively, affect national economic welfare—then the position is different. It would then be necessary to know whether the committee is also responsible for providing members with interpretations of expenditure plans in that vein. Or, in other words, whether 'economy' for the committee is to be given a 'Gladstonian' or a 'Keynesian' interpretation. Up to the present time 'Gladstonians' have won the day. Possibly one reason why an economist has not formally been appointed to the committee, is the Executive's fear that he may direct members' interests towards the Keynesian vision.

It is significant that both the Select Committee on Nationalised Industries and the Estimates Committee have found their common-sense advisers—intelligent amateurs—in the officials of the House. With two officials helping the former and one attached to each sub-committee of the latter, plus one for the plenary committee, there has, of late, been increasing satisfaction with the results achieved. All the officials are university graduates (some have read economics) and some have had twenty to thirty years' experience in committee-room politics in Parliament. As clerks to the committees, they guide the chairmen in varying degrees, they supply members with questions, they prepare draft reports, and their thinking sometimes has a profound effect upon the ultimate recommendations made. Perhaps the existing influence of the clerks to the committees, and their potential in this respect, inhibits the creation of 'expert' secretariats. What is really needed at the present time is not a reform in staffing arrangements, but a rationalisation of intention in the working of all three of the financial select committees. As they function at present, each goes its own way and there is an overlap of interests.[1] There is, in effect, some confusion of purpose—individually and collectively—and their formal terms of reference are an inadequate guide to their behaviour. Until 'purpose' is clarified the issue of expert assistance for the committees is hypothetical.[2]

The select committees and policy

Students of organisational arrangements will not be surprised that the carefully drafted terms of reference for the three committees are in each case inadequate definitions of their real contribution to government. With one committee formally limited to 'accounts', the second to recommending economies that are consistent with 'policy implied' in the Estimates, and the third looking at 'accounts and reports', they all look to be innocuous in the political sense. But the reality is different.

All three committees work extensively in the field of policy. Indeed, the mythical dichotomy between policy and administration bedevils a clear understanding of their potential. In public affairs one man's administration is another man's policy and this has led to a situation where each committee's scope for enquiry has been a matter of individual interpretation. And, as with most institutional arrangements, the character and the contribution of each committee have been determined as much by its personnel—their personalities, their social values, and their differing responses to political situations —as by the formal terms of reference. 'No power on earth', claimed the Chairman of the Public Accounts Committee in 1946, 'can stop

1. See the remarks on the overlapping interests of the Public Accounts and Estimates Committees by Sir G. Nicholson (Chairman of Estimates Committee 1961–4), 650 H C Deb., 5s., c. 658.
2. As from 1966 the question of expert assistance is to be referred to a new 'House of Commons Services Committee' including, amongst others, the Leader of the House, the Government Chief Whip and 'their equivalents on the Opposition side'. See Rt. Hon. H. W. Bowden, 718 H C Deb., 5s., c. 186, c. 879.

a Select Committee of the House of Commons from going beyond its terms of reference.'[1] And that was not an isolated threat of an eccentric committee leader. More recently, a Chairman of the Estimates Committee asserted: 'The committee has power to interpret its terms of reference and so to determine its scope for operation as it pleases.'[2] And in 1955 the Attorney-General (Sir Reginald Manningham Buller) told the preliminary Select Committee on Nationalised Industries '. . . that it is for the Committee to determine what is the proper construction to be placed on its own terms of reference . . .'.[3] In the light of the indefinite restraints that 'terms of reference' offer, front benches on both sides of the House have been reluctant to yield to the sporadic back-bench pressures, and also to assertions by authors of academic studies, to increase the number and the range of select committees. No doubt the terms of reference of the three financial select committees are the datum line for their respective activities; but a true measurement of their contribution in government should take account of additional factors such as people, politics, time and place.

Mention has been made of the changing function of the Public Accounts Committee. In this respect the Comptroller and Auditor-General has acknowledged publicly that in addition to its formal role of reconciling parliamentary appropriations with departmental accounts, the committee now has interests in securing 'value for money in public expenditure'. Indeed, one chairman (Harold Wilson) recently alleged it is now an 'elemental fallacy' to consider that the committee '. . . looks only to the past and is concerned only with inquests on a financial corpse'. As a consequence of the ongoing significance of public expenditure Wilson found that the Public Accounts Committee's interests 'are directly relevant to the current . . . and future spending activities'.[4] That committee's intrusion into matters related to the 'open ended' contracts for research and development on guided missiles has had, and will continue to

1. Mr Osbert Peake, HC 189-1 (Session 1945-6), Q. 4091.
2. *Public Administration* (Summer 1962), vol 40, p. 157.
3. HC 120 (Session 1955-6), Q. 7.   4. 632 HC Deb., 5s., cc. 897-8.

have, profound effects on future expenditure and contractual policy in that field, and the committee has been widely applauded for it.

It is much the same with the Estimates Committee. It would be hamstrung if it pursued the literal interpretation of its commission to secure economies 'consistent with policy'. Sir Frank Tribe—once Comptroller and Auditor-General—observed that '. . . it is very difficult to criticise an Estimate without dealing, at least to some extent, with the policy implied therein'.[1] In 1960 Lord Hinching-brooke was concerned that the committee was becoming a 'policy-maker' at the expense of continuing 'with its duties as a watchdog on public expenditure'.[2] And upon the committee's recommendation for the merger of the Colonial Office with the Commonwealth Relations Office, the Minister for Colonies (Mr Ian Macleod) called for '. . . a definition of policy at some time because if those . . . recommendations . . . are not policy I cannot see what else they are'.[3] That recommendation also prompted a disillusioned Professor J. D. B. Miller to write that the committee was '. . . more interested in getting its own policy adopted than in scrutinising estimates', and that 'it did not behave as any of the textbooks say the Estimates Committee either does or is supposed to behave'.[4] The committee's unpredictable behaviour was illustrated again by its enquiry in 1963–4 into 'Military Expenditure Overseas'. This took a sub-committee to a wide selection of overseas bases 'to get a more balanced picture of this vast subject'. The visits, however, were made in the face of a declaration from the Leader of the House that the 'constitutional position' was that 'no formal sittings could be held overseas, no evidence could be taken, and the questions asked overseas had to be repeated to the Service Departments in London on the Members' return'. The travel overseas was not authorised or financed by the House, but, euphemistically, it was made on 'the invitation of the Secretary of State for Defence to individual

1. *Public Administration* (Winter, 1954), vol XXXII, p. 369.
2. 632 HC Deb., 5s., c. 998.   3. *ibid*, c. 1016.
4. *Public Administration* (Summer, 1961), vol 39, p. 179. And see the just rejoinder from the committee's chairman (Sir Geoffrey Nicholson), *ibid* (Summer, 1962), vol 40, pp. 151–7.

Members and Clerks'.[1] It seems that the terms of reference of the select committees will usually be interpreted in political situations; and in this respect the bargaining power of the committee chairmen —through their power of reporting, and public revelation—can be substantial.

It was, indeed, an underlying suspicion of the potential of a select committee operating in the field of nationalised industries that delayed the creation of such a body for many years. Lord Reith (Chairman of the BBC) spoke of the projected committee as being 'terrifying to the public corporations', and he agreed that although it 'might start as a friendly communicative body [it] might end up by investigating and controlling'.[2] The Executive's timidity towards the emergent committee was expressed in the original terms of reference (see above, page 98). The provision of anything less restrictive, claimed a Labour member, was '. . . to risk industrial McCarthyism and irresponsibility . . .'.[3] But there was widespread resistance to the restrictions imposed, and members made the issue one of principle. They won new terms of reference which were drafted on the premise that 'We must leave it to the good sense and good will of the Committee to try to work out its own principles and rules as it goes along'.[4] Accordingly that committee, each session, is formally commissioned to '. . . examine the Reports and Accounts of the Nationalised Industries established by Statute . . .'. On the face of things any matter not mentioned in a corporation's report, or in its accounts, is not a matter for the committee. But the reality is different. The committee's major contribution has been made through its exploration of the formal and informal relationships that exist between a governing board of an industry and the responsible Minister. The committee has complained repeatedly of the blurred responsibility in this respect. It has sought clarification, and in its reports has philosophised on the respective roles of the

1. HC 302 (Session 1963–4), p. v. For further details see HC 162 (Session 1964–5), p. 4, and HC 303 (Session 1965–6), p. viii.
2. HC 235 (Session 1952–3), QQ. 611 and 678.
3. Mr Ronald Williams, 561 HC Deb., 5s., c. 622.
4. Mr H. Watkinson (Minister of Transport and Civil Aviation), *ibid*, c. 653.

relevant Minister, the Parliament and the public enterprise. The committee has objected to the 'Gentleman's Agreement' in the coal industry, whereby the Minister of Power has exercised control over fuel prices; it has objected to the Minister's informal interference in gas-industry tariffs; and it has complained of the non-statutory control exercised by the Minister over the Air Corporation, and asserted that it would be better for the Minister to act by formal 'directives'. Indeed, the chairman recently claimed that 'there is no prospect of getting good management and good leadership in the nationalised industries unless there are clear lines of responsibility between the Minister and the Chairman'.[1] Although very little has been done by the Executive in this respect, the committee's enquiries, and reports, have provided a great deal of discussion and a wider understanding of political motives in effecting public administration through statutory corporations. The committee has contributed much more to government than its terms of reference would suggest.[2]

Obviously, a great deal remains to be revealed about the functioning and the effects of these three select committees. It is now more than a decade since the publication of Professor Chubb's intensive enquiry into the work of two of them. There have been important developments since then, and a widening gap in the general understanding of their influence. Comments in this study on the possibilities for new select committees, or about reforms to strengthen the powers of those existing, are matters appropriate to the conclusions (Chapter 6). But before then there is need to look at the other side of the public bank account, to see what the House of Commons does in effecting its responsibilities to 'control' public revenue.

---

1. 698 H C Deb., 5s., cc. 532–3.
2. There is a valuable summary of the committee's work up to 1961, in *Reports of former select committees on nationalised industries*, etc., H C 116 (Session 1961–2).

5

RAISING THE REVENUE

'Parliamentary control of the Purse' implies control of public revenue as well as expenditure. The political significance of a government's revenue-raising policies, and the importance to democracy of parliamentary revenue control are beyond question. Indeed it is a feature of British Government that the major parliamentary-Executive conflicts over the centuries, that have helped to shape the British Constitution, have centred on issues about taxation rather than expenditure. And in the democratic conditions of the mid-twentieth-century politicians have recognised that a taxpayer's hip-pocket nerve is his most sensitive, that it has a direct link with the ballot box, and that they ignore it at their peril. It is understandable, therefore, that the procedures used in the House for the control of revenue by elected members have not been immune from party-political pressures, and that they could not be explained adequately as 'House of Commons matters'. They have all accrued from political situations, and in modern conditions they reflect the growing power of party oligarchies in the House.

A predominant feature of the procedures for revenue business at Westminster is the breadth of support they receive. Or, conversely, member dissatisfaction has not yet triggered-off backbench pressures strong enough to give rise to small select committees with revenue-raising interests, like those established for expenditure business. Attempts have been made to send the Finance

Bill (the annual taxing bill) upstairs to the standing committees, rather than hold it in a Committee of the Whole House, but they have failed. For its debate on revenue proposals the House perseveres (or has been made to persevere) as a plenary body, and it observes all four of Campion's rules.

Revenue raising in modern government depends upon taxation and borrowing. Constitutional purists would claim that the Parliament is sovereign in both—that it sanctions all changes in the revenue laws; for them the image of King Charles's head looms large. But, once more, the reality is different. The unprecedented expansion of the functions and the responsibilities of the State over the last century has necessitated substantial delegations to the Executive, by statute, of borrowing and revenue-raising powers. This is a well-recognised trend and, in spite of soundings of alarm, it is likely to continue. Instead of a comprehensive power of prior sanction over every change in the revenue law, the Commons, in cases where it has delegated its authority, has left itself only a retrospective veto over Executive Orders.

Delegation to the Executive of power to vary taxes began on a substantial scale in 1932 with the Parliament's approval of a comprehensive tariff in the Import Duties Act (since re-enacted in the Import Duties Act 1958). This step, said to be 'the wreath Neville Chamberlain laid on his father's tomb', established the mechanism for a virtual Executive control over tariff rates. In this the House of Commons held on to a power of veto that could be invoked 'within twenty-eight sitting days' after an Order was made, but it as much as surrendered its legislative power in tariff matters. And, more recently, the Executive gained the power to vary purchase tax. The Finance Act 1948 gave it authority to vary, by Order, classification of goods subject to purchase tax, or to substitute any statutory rate of tax for any other rate in respect of goods of any class. And, since 1961, that power has been extended to give the Chancellor of the Exchequer authority to vary any rate of purchase tax, to the extent of 10 per cent, up or down, conditional only upon retrospective parliamentary approval.

With borrowing, the position is much the same. In some cases authority for loan raising has been delegated to the Executive, and in others prior parliamentary approval remains necessary. Although a recent official review entitled 'Reform of the Exchequer Accounts' concluded that 'the Government has no specific powers to borrow to meet more than an insignificant part of its own direct capital expenditure . . .',[1] the Executive at present has statutory authority to raise loans through the Local Loan Funds for local authorities, for the provision of capital for the Post Office and the nationalised industries, and also for financing expenditure on New Towns. In these cases the Treasury, within prescribed limits, 'has complete discretion as to the forms and terms of borrowing'. Furthermore, the Treasury, under the National Loans Act 1939, has power 'to provide funds with which to repay an existing loan falling due or to fund a part of the Floating Debt . . . and to support the continuous process by which new Treasury Bills are issued to replace those falling due'. In the latter case the Treasury has 'complete discretion as to the type and terms of securities to be issued'.[2]

The power of Britain's Executive in revenue matters is, therefore, strong. And it is strengthened further by the practice of levying taxation permanently. Except for the income tax—an important exception, for it amounts to about 40 per cent of the total of revenue raised—all taxing statutes apply, year after year, until the Parliament, or the Executive, determines otherwise. It is not necessary for the Executive in raising its revenue to approach the Parliament annually for the approval in legislation of every detail of its taxing plan. It needs approval each year for only its proposed rates of income taxation, for new taxes, and for those adjustments it wishes to make to existing taxes which only Parliament can alter. As long as existing non-income taxes remain unchanged they do not run the gauntlet of annual political attack in a legislative process.

In this chapter interest will be focussed upon the methods used in

1. Cmnd 2014, p. 8.
2. Sir Herbert Brittain, *The British Budgetary System* (Allen and Unwin, 1959), pp. 178–9.

I

legislating for income taxation each year and for those other taxes that require prior authorisation in statute. But inextricably merged with the procedures for revenue approval, and adding to their complexity, is the phenomenon of the Executive's annual budget. It is difficult to separate the budget from the House's methods of revenue scrutiny. As some American students of public finance observed half a century ago, 'one cannot possibly understand the significance of the English budgetary procedure until he appreciates the fact that the interests of Parliament and the people centres on the receipt and not on the expenditure side of the budget'.[1] That still holds.

In a procedural sense it can be said that the budget of the British Government has been subordinated to its revenue component. No procedure has been designed specifically for its consideration as a comprehensive and basic annual financial unit. Debate in the House on the budget is tacked on to the annual debate on the revenue proposals it comprises. Indeed, the House has refused to acknowledge formally that a financial unit such as a budget exists. There is no provision for it, or even reference to it, in the Standing Orders, and there is no specific record in the Journals of the House of a budget ever having been presented. The House still recognises in its financial procedures only expenditure proposals (Supply) and revenue proposals (Ways and Means). Although John Morley could see that in Gladstone's day '. . . budgets are not really affairs of arithmetic, but in a thousand ways go to the root of the prosperity of individuals, the relation of classes and the strength of kingdoms'[2] the House has retained its pre-Gladstonian procedural blinkers to hide that fact. It has preserved what Aneurin Bevan once said were 'the conventions of a pastoral society', and regards the budget as 'an annual set of accounts'.[3]

Ironically, with the passing of time, the Commons have been shown to be half right, for the days of the annual budget as a

1. W. F. Willoughby, W. W. Willoughby and S. M. Lindsay, *The System of Financial Administration in Great Britain* (Appleton, 1917), p. 266.

2. J. Morley, *The Life of William Ewart Gladstone* (Macmillan, 1905), vol I, p. 458.

3. Referred to by Chancellor of the Exchequer (Mr Reginald Maudling), see 675 HC Deb., 5s., c. 454.

significant financial unit are receding. It brings undue rigidity into the finances of modern government. Instead, 'forward looks' have become fashionable, and the system of annual cash accounting is being subordinated to wider concepts of resource allocation. Possibly there is a diminishing need for the Commons formally to acknowledge in its financial procedures that an annual budget exists, but granted that, there are still serious deficiencies if the methods of the House relate only to the Executive's annual cash expenditure needs as balanced against its annual revenue-raising plan. This is the position at present. No provision has been made for a methodical debate of any financial plan, whatever its duration.

The House, therefore, relies solely upon debate for its control of revenue policy; and, as in expenditure business, its methods are best explained by following the application of the four financial rules.

Campion's four rules

In summary, the first of Campion's rules secures for the Executive the monopoly rights of financial initiative for all new and increased taxation and loan charges; the second provides that all such proposals will receive preliminary examination in a Committee of the Whole House—the Committee of Ways and Means; the third provides that all charges upon the people will be authorised by statute; and the fourth separates by time-delays the several stages of the legislative process.

Rule 1. Strict observance of the first rule is the principal means by which the formal power of the representative body in its determination of revenue policy has been weakened. In this respect the interpretations given the rule during the last century have been crucial. In view of the reference in the Standing Order of 1713 (at present No. 82) only to proposals that entail 'a grant or charge upon the public revenue', a great deal of verbal gymnastics has been necessary to secure the rule's application to proposals for imposing 'a charge upon the people'.

When the budgets were 'affairs of arithmetic', before universal suffrage, and when the purpose of raising revenue was simply to meet the Government's expenditure, the Executive's right of initiative in this sphere was based on the reasoning that the Crown's extraordinary expenditure needs gave rise to the occasional need to levy taxation. Although members acknowledged the Executive's rights to initiate the necessary revenue-raising proposals, they also claimed that, as legislators, they had a direct say in the subjects of taxation—Erskine May always contended in his *Parliamentary Practice* that 'the Crown had no concern in the nature and distribution of taxes'.[1] And May's contemporary, Alpheus Todd, put the situation just as clearly, if less precisely:

When the House resolves itself into a Committee of Ways and Means to consider of raising supplies for the service of the current year, it is competent for any member to propose another scheme of taxation for the same purpose as a substitute for the government plan.[2]

But values changed, just as the bases of representation in the House changed, and governments became increasingly sensitive about financial ideas other than their own, particularly if they were likely to have political appeal, and more particularly if they were expressed as proposals to amend taxing legislation. By mid-nineteenth century it had become evident that the admission of proposals for raising alternative sources of revenue would call for Ministers to declare attitudes in the division lobbies—and that could be politically embarrassing. Rulings from the chair in this respect increasingly favoured authority, and modern editions of Erskine May have rationalised the new interpretations of the rule with a tinge of piety:

The alteration of the practice was not deliberately adopted by the House, but seems to have imposed itself on the Chair through an instinctive appreciation of the fact that it was implied in the principle of the financial initiative of the Crown.[3]

1. Erskine May, *Parliamentary Practice* (first edition, 1844), p. 324; (ninth edition, 1883), p. 651. (May died in 1886, and the assertion was removed from the tenth edition.)

2. Alpheus Todd, *op. cit.*, vol 1, p. 451; and see Todd's reference to the freedom allowed members to propose increases to the tariff.

3. Erskine May, *op. cit.* (seventeenth edition, 1964), p. 733.

Today a position has been reached where the Executive claims not only all rights of original jurisdiction in increased taxation but it has convinced Clerks of the House that '. . . if an amendment might under any conceivable circumstance involve one single person in paying more tax it is out of order'.[1]

It is not difficult to recognise that the altered interpretations of the rule in the nineteenth and twentieth centuries have been restrictive upon private-member aspirations. But the effects of the rule upon private members were less stringent than in expenditure business, where the frustrations caused by the tendencies to move for increased spending, and the restraints of the rule, are notorious. On the revenue side, the urges of members to move for increased taxation are not nearly as widespread—although urges to change its incidence may be. In taxation business, members still have, and use, the scope to move for a wide range of tax reductions. This latitude, although it displays the arbitrariness of the rule—for member-initiated reductions of taxation could have social consequences equally as serious as member-initiated increases—has meant that the procedures for revenue business have caused less dissatisfaction. Indeed one uncompromising critic of the House of Commons of the 1930's, Professor Ramsay Muir, concluded 'so far as Ways and Means are concerned the system is not open to very serious criticism . . .'.[2] And a critic of the 1950's, Dr Paul Einzig, concluded that 'Parliamentary control of taxation has long ceased to be a problem from a constitutional point of view . . .'.[3] Notwithstanding these assurances, a closer look at the effect of the other rules in revenue business will show that there is less cause for complacency than these commentators would imply.

Rule 2. The application of the second rule to revenue business finds clear expression in the old Commons' resolution of 1667 which, since 1852, has had Standing Order authority (at present No. 87). It provides:

1. Sir Edward Fellowes, HC 110 (Session 1957), Q. 240.
2. HC 161 (Session 1930–1), p. 258, para. 10.   3. Paul Einzig, *op. cit.*, p. 325.

If any motion be made in the House for any . . . charge upon the people, the consideration and debate thereof shall not be presently entered upon . . . it shall be referred to a committee of the whole House before any resolution or vote of the House do pass therein.

To meet the provisions of this Order the Committee of Ways and Means is established early in every session with terms of reference 'to consider of the ways and means for raising the supply to be granted to Her Majesty'. These terms, on pre-Keynesian values, suggest a dependence in the work of the committee on earlier determinations of the Committee of Supply. Hatsell expressed this link, as he understood it, late in the eighteenth century:

that the money proposed to be raised upon the subject by loans or taxes, or any other mode, should not exceed the sum already granted in Committee of Supply.[1]

The historic Supply–Ways and Means nexus is still considered to exist; it continues to find expression in Erskine May to the effect that there is an 'established principle' that 'no more money should be raised by taxation than is necessary to cover the supply already voted by, or at any rate demanded from, the House of Commons'.[2] But, in reality, there is no attempt by the House to strike an equation or to impose any quantitative limitations on revenue raising. The direct interdependence of the two committees is fictional. This, however, does not alter the fact that every charge upon the people coming before the House of Commons starts its parliamentary journey in the Committee of Ways and Means. There is still a strict observance of Rule 2 in that respect.

But the observance of a rule of procedure, and the pursuit of its intended purpose, are not necessarily synonymous. The Committee of Ways and Means has become a mere façade hiding the reality of Executive power; and in many respects this development has been inevitable. In the case of almost every revenue proposal emanating

1. Hatsell, *op. cit.*, vol III, p. 196.
2. Erskine May, *op. cit.* (seventeenth edition, 1964), p. 720.

from the Executive there is an accompanying necessity for its immediate application so as to obviate forestalling action on the part of the less co-operative taxpayers. As a result it has been necessary to curtail preliminary debate on taxing proposals and, hence, preclude the reasoned determination of the decision to tax that Rule 2 was intended to provide. The Executive's need in modern times is for the House to come to a taxing resolution promptly. As Stanley Baldwin once explained:

after any change in taxation became known outside and there were any delay in making the change effective, the revenue would run a chance of losing, it might be millions, and a number of worthy people whom it is not our part to make wealthy at our expense, would profit considerably.[1]

To make an alteration in taxation effective, without delay, governments in the nineteenth century adopted the practice of assuming that a resolution of the Committee of Ways and Means gave sufficient provisional authority for immediate tax collections until such time as expression was given to that resolution in law. But the levy, and the collection of taxation on the authority of a mere resolution of a single House of the Parliament, were open to question; the practice found its critics. Erskine May as early as 1863 claimed 'it is obvious that it is not strictly legal'.[2] And in the financial crisis in 1909 over the Lords rejection of Lloyd George's Finance Bill, its legal insecurity became patently clear. The practice escaped formal challenge, however, until 1912 when ex-Conservative MP T. Gibson Bowles, incensed at increased levies being made, without clear statutory authority, on dividends from his Irish land stock, sought the protection of the High Court. Bowles alleged that the practice was an infringement of both the Petition of Right and the Bill of Rights, and the Court found in his favour:

a resolution of the Committee of the House of Commons for Ways and Means, assenting to income tax at a certain rate for the ensuing financial

1. 256 HC Deb., 5s., c. 180.
2. Erskine May, *op. cit.* (fifth edition, 1863), pp. 534–5.

year does not . . . authorise the Crown to levy on the subject the tax so assented to before the tax has been actually imposed by Act of Parliament.[1]

To meet the inconvenience of *Bowles v. Bank of England* Lloyd George (as Chancellor of the Exchequer) introduced in 1912, and Parliament passed in 1913, the Provisional Collection of Taxes Bill to preserve the old practice (with qualifications) under the authority of statute. Significantly, the new Act gave a legal expression to Rule 2; it vested taxing resolutions with the authority of law when 'passed by the Committee of Ways and Means of the House of Commons (so long as it is a Committee of the Whole House)'.[2] In some respects it provided reforms like those Balfour introduced into expenditure business in 1896, by bringing time-limitations into the legislative process for raising revenue. It provided that the provisional authority vested in a taxing resolution 'shall cease to have statutory effect' if the resolution is not adopted by the House within ten sitting days, if the second reading of the subsequent bill is not passed within twenty sitting days of the resolution, and if the bill's passage took longer than four months. The Act still applies, and with the taxing proposals of a modern government normally presented early every April, it means that the annual Finance Bill must be passed by early August, or the provisional authority will lapse. There is, however, one important exception—the Act does not apply to new subjects of taxation. They, although infrequent, have to await the full course of the legislative process before they can legally be collected.

The Provisional Collection of Taxes Act, however, did not declare that the Committee of Ways and Means shall come to a taxing resolution immediately. That remained at the discretion of the House. It was not until 1947 that the immediate resolution of tax proposals in the Committee of Ways and Means became mandatory by Standing Order. That Order, although it declared practice, formally and finally negated the true financial and pre-

1. *Bowles v. Bank of England* [1913], 1 ch. 57 (Notes). And see *Bowles v. Bank of England:* the proceedings and official court documents (Butterworth, 1914).
2. 3 and 4 Geo. V., ch. 3.

liminary purpose of the committee. Forced through by a Labour Government, contrary to the recommendation of a Select Committee on Procedure, the Standing Order left the form of the Committee of Ways and Means but robbed it of its substance. And to add insult to injury it also proscribed debate at the succeeding stage, when the undebated resolutions were reported to the House. The double proscription still applies (at present Standing Order No. 90). It warrants full quotation:

(1) When a Minister of the Crown in Committee of Ways and Means has made the first of several motions upon which a bill is to be founded for imposing, renewing, varying or repealing any charge upon the people, the chairman shall forthwith put the question thereupon and shall then successively put forthwith the question on each further motion made by the Minister, save the last motion.

(2) On consideration of a resolution reported from the Committee of Ways and Means for imposing, renewing, varying or repealing a charge upon the people, the question 'That this House doth agree in the said resolution' shall be put forthwith.

This Standing Order applies to instances when there are 'several motions', which is the case on occasions for implementing the revenue proposals of an annual or a 'supplementary' budget. In accordance with the Order, the Chancellor of the Exchequer moves, and the committee immediately resolves, on all but the 'last motion'. The latter is known as the 'amendment of the law' motion: it does not impose a tax. This sole unresolved motion is the procedural point for the annual budget debate—'a general debate ... on the broadest lines'—where members may 'consider expenditure in its relation to the burden of providing the necessary revenue';[1] it lasts about four sitting days and, formally, gives the House the opportunity to veto the budget as a unit (after the taxes have been provisionally approved). But in no sense is the budget debate the occasion to determine the details of taxation.

In revenue business, therefore, the advantages of Rule 2 have been

1. Erskine May, *op. cit.* (seventeenth edition, 1964), p. 819.

foreclosed, not by the subtle procedural techniques used in expenditure business, but by the blatant prohibitions of any preliminary debate on taxation details.

Rule 3. Since Gladstone in 1861 responded to the House of Lords' rejection of one of the taxing measures of his budget, by integrating the revenue proposals of the annual budget into one omnibus bill—at first the Customs and Inland Revenue Bill, but since 1894 the Finance Bill—the legislative process for taxation (in accordance with Rule 3) has gained unity. This has meant that the prohibition placed upon the preliminary debate on taxation detail has had the effect of concentrating member participation, and interest, into the several stages of the subsequent enacting bill.

The Finance Bill pursues the conventional legislative process of first and second readings, the committee and report stages, and the third reading, and all these stages are taken on the floor of the House. Even the detailed committee stage, by Standing Order (at present No. 40), is not permitted to be taken elsewhere.

Introduced to give statutory effect to the resolutions of the Committee of Ways and Means the Finance Bill has a preamble with a little irony, it reads:

Most Gracious Sovereign—
We Your Majesty's most dutiful and loyal subjects, the Commons of the United Kingdom in Parliament assembled, towards raising the necessary supplies to defray your Majesty's public expenses, and making an addition to the public revenue, have freely and voluntarily resolved to give and grant unto your Majesty the several duties hereinafter mentioned . . .

In keeping with the notion of taxation being the House's free and voluntary gift, the name of the Chairman of the Committee of Ways and Means precedes the names of several Treasury Ministers as those initiating the bill.

Upon its introduction, after the Committee of Ways and Means resolutions have been agreed to on report, the Finance Bill is read a first time, ordered to be printed, and the second reading debate set-down for the 'next day'. Of one day's duration, the second reading debate is usually a repetition of the budget debate; Sir Gilbert Campion once said that expenditure could be discussed '. . . not entirely on its own; not merely as items of expenditure, but as a balance between expenditure and revenue as a whole'.[1] The decks are quickly cleared for the Finance Bill's committee stage.

The House of Commons has preserved vestiges of its classical role as a legislature in its committee consideration of the Finance Bill. With aspirations less restricted by Rule 1 than is the case in expenditure business, members have freedom to propose amendments for a wide range of reductions to proposed taxation. There is widespread participation. The absence of the Executive's parrot-cry of 'vote of confidence' on every proposal, and its preparedness to yield to pressure and accept amendments, make for a markedly different debating atmosphere. Members participate openly in proposing amendments in the interests of outside organisations as well as constituents. The debate on the bill has become increasingly popular: four or five days each year were given to the committee stage of the Finance Bill in the period of the Labour Government 1946–50, and in the period of Conservative Governments, 1951–62, an average of nine days was absorbed, with the initiative in proposing amendments coming from both sides.[2] In the opinion of the Labour Party Whip in 1963 'This is one bill of the year where there is a great deal of public interest, and we are faced by letters and communications about different sections . . .'.[3] In one day's consideration of the Finance Bill in 1952, 190 proposed amendments and thirty-five proposed new clauses stood on the Order Paper for selection and consideration.[4] In the Finance Bill in 1957 some 285 amendments were 'put down', of which twenty-eight were government amendments, and the names of 272 members backed the rest.[5]

1. HC 189–I (Session 1945–6), Q. 2199.
2. See 'Time spent on Finance Bills, 1946–62', HC 190 (Session 1962–3), p. 23.
3. Rt. Hon. H. W. Bowden, *ibid*, Q. 38.
4. Tregear, A. A., *House of Commons—Procedure*, Australian Parliamentary Paper no. 200 (Session 1952–3), p. 11.
5. Sir Edward Fellowes, HC 92–I (Session 1958–9), Q. 88. (Only sixty-six were eventually called and they were moved by thirty-seven individual members.)

In 1961, 175 members spoke at the committee stage and in 1962, 173.[1] And in 1965, Labour's controversial Finance Bill, introducing a Capital Gains Tax and a new Corporation Tax, occupied the House for twenty-one and a half sitting days (211 hours) and provoked 1,222 amendment proposals (680 from the Conservative Opposition and 440 from the Chancellor of the Exchequer).[2]

It is to be expected that the degree of legislative activity on the Finance Bill calls for stringent controls, and in keeping with the tenor of other branches of financial procedure, these have not been lacking. There are two techniques of particular importance.

The first control over member participation stems from the use of the Ways and Means resolutions (mainly determined without debate) as the financial criterion for the subsequent legislative process. As with expenditure business, the Executive has shown a capacity to draft taxing resolutions restrictively so as to limit the scope for amendment proposals. Current editions of Erskine May explain the potential of a Ways and Means resolution in this respect:

Amendments [i.e. proposed amendments] must not exceed the scope, increase the amount or extend the incidence of any charge upon the people, defined by the terms of the ways and means resolution, as agreed to by the House . . .[3]

The advantages to the Executive in having both the Ways and Means stage and the report stage free of debate are therefore obvious. The House, then, is restricted by terms that the Executive dictates. But when Sir Stafford Cripps in 1949 wanted to limit the scope of debate on the Finance Bill of that year, it was to his credit that he included the expression of his restriction in the 'Amendment of the law' resolution—which was debatable. Cripps drafted the resolution so as to preclude the introduction of amendments on the purchase tax. He claimed that the prohibition was necessary 'to enable industry to get away from the embarrassing

---

1. HC 190 (Session 1962–3), p. iii, and Q. 72.   2. 716 HC Deb., 5s., c. 805.
3. Erskine May, *op. cit.* (seventeenth edition, 1964), p. 826.

situation in which they did not know whether in the course of the
Finance Bill there was to be some reduction or not'.[1] Only one
member of the Opposition detected Cripps's manœuvre but his cry
went unanswered. And subsequently, when inconvenienced by the
restriction, the Opposition alleged that Cripps had used 'a new
means of preventing the expression in the House of the intense feeling that obtains outside in relation to the incidence of Purchase
Tax'.[2] The means was not new—it was analogous to a Money
Resolution—and it has been used on many occasions since, but as a
controlling technique in debate on taxation business it was a development of first importance. It is something to be reflected upon, particularly by those who wish to abolish the Committee of Ways and
Means.

The second technique for control, generally accepted by members
as inevitable, is the use by the Chairman of Ways and Means of the
'kangaroo' procedure for selecting from the amendments proposed
by members those to be brought before the committee for consideration. Although not an overt Executive control over the House,
this is a limitation that the Executive condones. Only about one in
every four amendments 'put down' by members is selected for
debate and decision. The selection method, therefore, is a significant
part of the political process.

In 1963 the Chairman of Ways and Means (Sir William
Anstruther-Gray) explained that in selecting amendments he was
assisted by 'the Deputy Chairman of Ways and Means, the Clerk
Assistant, the Second Clerk Assistant, the Clerk of Public Bills, the
Clerk to the Chairman of Ways and Means . . . and also the Government Draftsman'.[3] The general aim he said is 'to spread the net as
widely as possible to let every interest of those who have a particular
interest in the Finance Bill to get a hearing . . .'. He arranged conferences in his room with 'sectional' interests about amendments and
new clauses. And, significantly, he claimed '. . . I consult with who-
ever is in charge of the Bill on the Opposition side as to which

1. 465 HC Deb., 5s., c. 567.   2. 463 HC Deb., 5s., c. 2720.
3. HC 190, *op. cit.*, Q. 70.

amendments, say, to attach particular importance . . . and which are not so important . . .'.[1]

As a result of the widespread and increasing number of members participating in the committee stage of the Finance Bill, and the parliamentary time it consumes, pressure has been exerted over recent years for the delegation of the responsibility for its scrutiny to small and less cumbersome committees. The issue was referred to the Select Committe on Procedure in 1959 which concluded 'The greatest single economy that could be produced in the time spent on the floor of the House would be to commit the Finance Bill at least in part to a standing committee'.[2] This was received in the House with uncertainty on both sides, including the front benches. Economy in the use of time was seen as a high ideal but agreement was lacking as to whose interest was to be sacrificed in its name. The Committee in 1959 ambiguously left the decision 'to the House to be determined in the light of circumstances . . .'.[3] The problem received further attention from the Select Committee on Procedure in 1963 which, after examining the Leader of the House and the Chief Whips from both sides, yielded to '. . . a strong body of opinion which believes that even the committal of a part of the Bill would be a breach of constitutional principle, namely that the House as a whole must keep control over the executive in matters of taxation'. On that kind of reasoning the committee reported that it would '. . . not recommend that any part of the Finance Bill should be committed to a Standing Committee, even as an experiment'.[4]

Much, of course, can be wrapped-up in the blanket of 'constitutional principle'. The issue in 1963 displayed the clash of interests in the affairs of the House. A submission made by the Financial Secretary to the Treasury claimed that the change contemplated would sometimes make it 'impossible' for Treasury Ministers to prepare for afternoon and evening debates in the House, 'since they would be involved in the Committee in the mornings'.[5] The Government Chief Whip thought that an experiment would be

1. *ibid*, Q. 72.   2. HC 92–1, *op. cit.*, p. viii.   3. *ibid*, Q. ix.
4. HC 190, *op. cit.*, p. iv.   5. *ibid*, p. 26.

worth while if it is 'what the House wants'. But then he asked, rhetorically, 'who knows what the House wants?'.[1] The Opposition Chief Whip explained that under existing circumstances the 'usual channels' worked satisfactorily 'to a voluntary time-table'; and he admitted that 'it is not easy to visualise a position whereby either the Government or the Opposition get together and in fact speak for all the Back Benchers'.[2] Evidence, however, was not taken from back-bench members. Nor was consideration given to the prospect of designing a new form of committee machinery for this unique problem. The committee's focus of interest was on fitting debate into the existing arrangements and to suit front-bench interests.[3] The problem, therefore, remains—how a representative assembly may function effectively as a legislative body, particularly when a large part of its rank and file membership wants it to.

In spite of its prolonged consideration of the Finance Bill in the Committee of the Whole each year, the House has preserved the bill's report stage as a debatable procedural step. In theory further amendments may be moved. But in the opinion of the Chairman of Ways and Means in 1963, the airing of an amendment at that time 'is not really very satisfactory. It is too late for the Government to give a promise that they will think it over and maybe include it in the report'.[4] The stage usually lasts two days, and after it the bill's third reading is disposed of in a few hours, often on Friday, when attendance is sparse. The latter stage is used for valediction, when members from the Treasury bench speak with pride of their achievements in piloting the bill through, and it gives the Opposition their final opportunity to cast aspersions on the measure's principles—that is, within May's dictum that 'debate and amendment must be strictly relevant to the content of the bill'.[5]

Rule 4. It is notable in this branch of financial business, that there

1. Rt. Hon. M. Redmayne, *ibid*, Q. 28.   2. Rt. Hon. H. W. Bowden, *ibid*, Q. 61.
3. For subsequent enquiry and further front-bench resistance to change see HC 276 (Session 1964–5) and 718 HC Deb., 5s., cc. 172–296.
4. *ibid*, Q. 88.   5. Erskine May, *op. cit.* (seventeenth edition, 1964), p. 827.

is no Standing Order dispensation of Rule 4. Even though the report of the Ways and Means resolutions is now a formality, a time interval is insisted upon between it and the preceding stage. Sometimes, however, the rule is dispensed with by simple resolutions for a particular purpose, such as in 1954:

That the Finance Bill as amended, may be considered immediately after the recommittal of the Bill and report thereof, notwithstanding the practice of the House as to the interval between the various stages. . . .

The following is an example of the sequence of stages, and the interposition of the time intervals, that ensure that no tax measure is rushed through. The passage of the Finance Bill 1963 through the House of Commons was as follows:

3 April   Budget day

> Budget resolutions moved in the Committee of Ways and Means by the Chancellor of the Exchequer.

> All but the last of twenty-nine resolutions passed.

> General debate commenced on the 'Amendment of the Law' resolution, and continued 4, 8, and 9 April.

9 April   Last resolution passed

TIME INTERVAL

10 April   All budget resolutions reported to House.
> Finance Bill ordered to be brought in.

> Bill introduced (sixty-nine clauses and twelve schedules),

> First reading: day named for second reading.

	TIME INTERVAL
6 May	Second reading—moved, debated, and carried.
	TIME INTERVAL
16 May	Committee stage . . . continued 21, 23, 28, 29, and 30 May.
30 May	Bill reported to House with amendments.
	TIME INTERVAL
25 June	Bill re-committed, consideration continued 26 June.
26 June	Reported with amendments.
	TIME INTERVAL
28 June	Third reading.

The question of whether or not the time-interval principle is redundant in the conditions of modern government is difficult to answer. Like so many of the questions about parliamentary reform, or the suggestions for 'streamlining' or making parliamentary procedures 'businesslike', they usually express dilemmas about the lessening of the Parliament's capacity to offer resistance to the Executive's will. The question of the abolition of the time-interval principle in revenue business would involve the removal of a safeguard against rushed and ill-considered tax imposts. How far should reformists go in that direction? The issue, therefore, is part of a wider and fundamental problem—what is the role of the elected member in the legislative process in modern government? And that is a matter for the concluding chapter.

K

6

IS PARLIAMENTARY FINANCIAL CONTROL
A MYTH?

It is evident from the chapters above that the House of Commons has established two means of financial control. The first is the financial-legislative process based on the expression of the Bill of Rights that every financial charge—upon the people or upon the public revenue—shall be made by a 'grant of Parliament', and this is supplemented by the ancient practice of making all grants by statute. And the second is the use of select committees, with formally expressed terms of reference, permitting enquiry into subjects of financial significance and with responsibilities to report back to the House. The actual interdependence between the two means is, however, tenuous. In conclusion, therefore, the method here will be to review each in turn, to comment on some obvious deficiencies, and to consider what degree of financial control is, in fact, attained.

(i) THE FINANCIAL-LEGISLATIVE PROCESS

The financial-legislative process is characterised by its complexity. The technical jargon associated with the Committee of Supply, the Committee of Ways and Means, and Money Resolutions, is notoriously antique and abstruse. Criticisms are legion, and most are warranted. But the judgements so frequently made, that condemn the financial gibberish along with the traditional procedures, are apt to be arbitrary; indeed, they beg the important question of how control over the finances of the modern state may be exercised? For as complex and mysterious as the ancient methods appear they have that rationale that Campion has so ably expounded in four 'rules'. The advocates for the abolition of the ancient paraphernalia are noticeably reticent when it comes to advancing alternative methods or substitute 'rules'.

Fundamental to the case of the abolitionists is the solution of the problem—whether the House should or should not function as a legislative body when it comes to voting expenditure and approving taxation. If every financial charge is to be embodied in a statute, it is necessary to ask whether elected members are in fact to be the architects of the financial laws. Or, alternatively, is their legislative power in this respect to be simply the power of veto over Executive proposals?

There are many assertions that the House of Commons is unfitted to be a legislature in the sense of shaping the statute law—be it financial or otherwise. But there are counter-claims, and parliamentary records to support them, to the effect that elected representatives are capable, via a suitably designed legislative process, to play a responsible and constructive role in determining the provisions of the statute book. As a result, there is confusion.

Reference has already been made to the animated process in the House of Commons by which members approve and, to a degree, shape the annual Finance Bill. Moreover, students of the House can point to contemporary examples such as the London Government Bill, the Homicide Bill and the several bills for establishing the nationalised industries, to vindicate claims that the House may still work as a legislature in the classical sense. (Assessments of the value of the contribution that members make to particular statutes will, of course, always be subjective.) But the facts of member contributions to legislation fly in the face of John Stuart Mill's assertion 'that a numerous assembly is as little fitted for the direct business of legislation as for that of administration' and that the determination of law is the business of experts with minds 'trained to the task through long and laborious study'.[1] And Mill was not alone.

1. Mill, *op. cit.*, p. 168.

Bentham before him is said to have claimed 'that once legislation had been framed by the official law makers, it should be adopted by Parliament without amendment, or rejected altogether'.[1] Bentham and Mill held reservations about the political process in Parliament. For them, what was acceptable to an aristocratic House was not necessarily appropriate to a democratic one.

The fears of Mill and Bentham did not die with them, they linger on into the twentieth century. In 1912, for example, Sir Courtenay Ilbert acknowledged the problem—'of legislating through the agency of a representative and popular assembly, the necessity for which is admitted by every free country, has nowhere been satisfactorily solved . . .'.[2] About twenty years later, Professor Ivor Jennings pursued the Mill line with—'A popular assembly is not and cannot be a good legislature. Modern legislation dealing with complicated industrial matters or a vast organisation of social services is too technical for private members to contribute much to it . . .'.[3] And in 1951 Professor J. A. G. Griffith, on grounds of technicality, saw the modern function of Parliament in legislation to be simply 'examination, criticism and approval'.[4]

Elected members of the House of Commons, on the other hand, have other ideas. With fickle electorates to please and persistent interest groups to satisfy, and with a social status bolstered by their popular image as lawmakers, they are vigorous in resisting limitations to their legislative power. It was not entirely unexpected, therefore, that a Select Committee on Procedure in 1963 should insist that 'The right of the House to legislate as and when it pleases should not be limited'.[5]

What is confusing in the study of legislative behaviour in matters of finance is that the trend away from the classical legislative

1. Quoted in a review article attributed to Erskine May, *Edinburgh Review* (1854), vol 99, p. 277.
2. *Methods of Legislation* (University of London Press, 1912), p. 45.
3. Ivor Jennings, *Parliament must be reformed* (Kegan Paul, 1941), p. 42.
4. 'The Place of Parliament in the Legislative Process', *The Modern Law Review* (1951), vol 14, pp. 279–96 and 425–36. (This is the best contemporary examination of the problem that is published.)
5. HC 135 (Session 1962–3), p. v.

function varies in its extent with each category of financial business. This makes it difficult to recommend reforms that are based on 'rules', analagous to Campion's, and which are capable of general application.

In Supply debates, for example, members are in no sense the architects of current policy—even though the Supply procedures presume that they are. Financial control in the voting of expenditure estimates has become simply a veto control. Twenty-six 'allotted' Supply days each session provide occasions for debates on topical issues in party politics, some of which have only a vague relationship to the Estimates. But with Money Resolutions, and with taxation proposals, it is different; members still aspire to be legislators, in spite of the Executive's use of procedural techniques to keep their aspirations within limited bounds. It would be difficult for a reformer to change the ethos of member behaviour in those respects. It will be to advantage, therefore, to take each category of the financial-legislative process in turn.

Supply

Possibly the most productive field for reform in the financial procedures rests in the changes that could be effected to rationalise the Supply process. In this category of business members have already changed the purpose of debate but not the procedures for it. A stage has been reached where Supply business could now be exempted from Campion's four rules and a fresh start made without upheaval; and, indeed, with substantial advantage to Parliament, to the Executive and to the nation.

This is to presume, however, that the facts of Supply debate nowadays are enough to support a new theory. On empirical evidence, the function of the House at present in controlling expenditure through debating Estimates is simply to accept or reject expenditure proposals after political debate. If this is valid, then the complex methods that presume the minute examination by the whole House of financial statistics, are redundant. It would mean also that the Estimates and their associated documents are no longer a satisfactory basis for the debates that are held; moreover, members are now concerned with other facets of expenditure policy—for example, debt policy, the whole range of local-government expenditure, the income and outflow of the National Insurance Funds, or the expenditure-investment policies of the nationalised industries—none of which are adequately explained by the Estimates. What is needed in the House in current conditions are procedures that will provide opportunities for debates, during the course of the 'allotted' days, covering the whole range of public expenditures— in its entirety, section by section, or by individual projects. And such debates should be freed from the encumbrances to free expression that accompany the ancient Committee of Supply. And they should be supplemented by the provision to members of adequate explanatory material prepared in prose rather than in figures.

This is to assert, therefore, that the expenditure debates should not be part of the financial-legislative process. The subjects for debate ought still to be selected by the Opposition but the motions upon which they are conducted should be reasoned and meaningful expressions concerning policy, to which any member, or Minister, may put down alternative expressions as similarly reasoned and meaningful amendment proposals. And the scope in the selection of subject matter for debate on these occasions ought to be as wide as the scope of government.

Sceptics, and parliamentary romanticists, will ask what is to happen to the formal voting of Estimates and Supplementary Estimates and the related Consolidated Fund and Consolidated Fund (Appropriation) Bills? These financial units should be seen for what they are. They are nowadays the instruments of Executive rather than parliamentary control of finance; they are the bases of Treasury control of departmental cash expenditure and the annual cash audit by the Comptroller and Auditor-General (admittedly on behalf of Parliament). In no sense are they designed to make effective, or to facilitate, the House's debates on expenditure policy; indeed it could be argued that they are designed to weaken them; and that the cash-control they presuppose is an anachronism of the *laissez-faire* society of the 1850's when the saving of 'candle-ends' was the hall-mark of good government.

It is perfectly appropriate, therefore, that the approval of annual expenditure estimates and the passage of Consolidated Fund Bills should be mere formalities in the wake of extensive debate on party-political issues; and it is logical that they should be passed 'on the nod'. If there is to be any scrutiny of their detail, then that is the function of the financial select committees. The fact that the bills are accepted as formalities does not destroy the power of the House in times of political crisis to refuse to pass them.[1]

The above proposals, however, gloss over one of the serious problems of modern government—whether or not the elective body should have a prior control over the Executive's expenditure commitments. In other words, should the Executive be free to enter into commitments as and when it pleases and be subject only to a retrospective sanction by the House. This issue attracted the attention of Lord Plowden's enquiry into 'Control of Public Expenditure' in 1960–1, and about which his committee reported 'formidable difficulties'.

The Plowden Committee contended that parliamentary control of commitments would lead to a 'double system'—first, the authorisation of 'the amount to be spent each year' and, secondly, the approval of 'commitments to be undertaken in the year'. The latter 'are of many and different types and often span a number of years'. If prior control was to be maintained members would need 'long term expenditure surveys'. And the committee claimed that the government 'could hardly make its own surveys available'. Its conclusion, therefore, was 'it would be impossible to work efficiently any system of parliamentary control of commitments which went beyond what is already implied in the present processes of

---

1. This is largely the case put to the Select Committee on Procedure in 1965 by the Clerk Assistant of the House of Commons (Mr D. W. S. Lidderdale), viz. 'The House would . . . have a better chance of achieving an effective control of finance if it were . . . to abandon the pretence that it exercised such control through the Committee of Supply, and were instead to concentrate on the . . . use of Select Committees.' HC 303 (Session 1964–5), p. 8. Cf. Mr Balfour's statement of 1896, above, pp. 69–70.

Supply and legislation'. But, as to what those 'present processes' achieve, the Plowden report was silent.[1]

The British Executive's comparative freedom from prior parliamentary approval of expenditure projects was one of the major findings of Professor Samuel Beer's perceptive study of *Treasury Control* published in 1956. He found '. . . the British executive has wider freedom of movement [than the American executive] which may greatly facilitate making policy and inaugurating programmes'. And that 'Liabilities may be incurred . . . not only before appropriation has been made but also in the absence of a statute embodying a financial resolution'.[2] This conclusion makes nonsense of what was generally understood to be 'Parliamentary Control of Expenditure' and of contemporary notions such as Professor Christopher Hughes's that in Britain 'Parliament has a stranglehold over finance'.[3] It was to the credit of the Plowden enquiry in 1961 that it brought the essence of Beer's thesis into the open, and it stated categorically, via an official report, that Parliament no longer wields a comprehensive control over expenditure commitments.

It is becoming increasingly evident that under new conditions of government, parliamentary control of expenditure resides in the political sanctions that may be applied, retrospectively, through public debate and select committee enquiry. 'Control' via a prior parliamentary sanction of all expenditure proposals is a thing of the past. It ought to be acknowledged, however, that the Plowden Committee, in recognition of this, insisted that:

> . . . what is most important to Parliament is to have the opportunity to express a view on the scale and direction of big blocks of expenditure which are not suitable for detailed and individual Parliamentary control.[4]

Nowadays, methods are needed that will ensure that the political and the social implications of the Executive's expenditure policies

1. Cmnd 1432, *op. cit.*, pp. 23–4.
2. Samuel H. Beer, *Treasury Control* (OUP, second edition, 1957), pp. 50–2.
3. Christopher Hughes, *The Parliament of Switzerland* (Hansard Society, 1962), p. 136.
4. Plowden Committee, *op. cit.*, p. 28.

will be disclosed and debated publicly (albeit retrospectively) by means which will not obscure major facts in a maze of minor detail. Methods are needed that will facilitate systematic discussion in the House of Commons on the Executive's economic plans, and on its planning. The old presumptions about House of Commons control via debate about cash allocations are now due for scrapping. And the sooner the better for they bind mental attitudes to outmoded notions of government.

Money Resolutions

If the expenditure-granting processes are to be converted into formal and annually recurring opportunities for discussion on current political issues, then the question must be asked—what is to become of the Money Resolution procedure? This, it was noted in Chapter 3, is the technique for the Executive's restraint upon private-member initiative in cases where new legislation has expenditure implications. It provides for a subtle and restrictive application of Rule 1.

Obviously, the question of the retention of the Money Resolution, or its abolition, is closely related to the role of the elective body as a legislature. It can be used, at a Minister's discretion, in limitation of the legislative process. Its abolition, without alternative restrictions, would provide for increased political activity in passing legislation. But in view of the suspicions that party leaders hold towards an expansion of private-member liberty, that is a remote possibility. Possibly the solution adopted in Australia offers an alternative— there, the Money Resolution has been abolished in favour of Standing Orders that declare for Ministers of the Crown absolute monopoly rights over all financial initiative if it can be interpreted (usually by the Chairman of Committees on a Minister's advice) to bring an increased charge upon the people or upon the public revenue. This, of course, is to call upon the House, formally, to renounce a large part of its right to shape legislation. In Britain, where members continue to be legislators, this course is unlikely. The Money Resolution, it seems, will stay. But if that is so, the procedure should be acknowledged for what it is. The Money Resolution is not, as Dr Bernard

Crick alleges—'at best a cumbersome, and at worst an extremely time wasting device';[1] but it is, as Lord Campion explained—'. . . a neat and flexible instrument which can be nicely adjusted so as to allow the House just as much latitude in the criticism and amendment of the financial provisions of a bill *as Ministers think reasonable*'.[2]

Taxation

In turning to the revenue side of the financial picture—to the Finance Bill and the budget debate associated with it—there is a situation similar to that with Money Resolutions. With elected members insisting upon attempting to amend the revenue law as proposed by the Executive, techniques have been developed for restraining their enthusiasm. The resolutions of the Committee of Ways and Means are used to define the scope for initiative that members may exercise in the subsequent legislative stages. It is unlikely, therefore, that the Ways and Means stage will be abolished while members, during the process for enacting the tax law, seek to force their ideas about taxation upon the Chancellor of the Exchequer. And there is no doubt that the Executive will continue to offer the same restraint should the Finance Bill ever be sent upstairs to the Standing Committees. The fundamental question, therefore, once again, is whether or not members are to be legislators in approving the Executive's revenue proposals.

If members were to surrender their claims to be legislators in revenue matters—as they have done with Supply matters—then a procedure could be developed to enable general and prolonged (non-legislative) debates on revenue policy as a prelude to the formal 'on the nod' enactment of the Finance Bill. This would free the eight to ten days spent in shaping the details of the Finance Bill for wider political debate, unaffected by the restrictions that Rule 1 imposes. But, again, such a change is unlikely. There are political satisfactions for elected members in having, or striving to have, the taxation burden lightened; whereas, in contrast, there is little political satisfaction in having the expenditure burden lightened.

1. *op. cit.*, p. 81.   2. HC 189-1 (Session 1945-6), p. xxvii. (Italics added.)

Members will for long reject the claims of Bentham, Mill, and Jennings about the House's shortcomings as a legislature when it comes to matters of taxation. What will probably happen in the direction of reform in this sphere is that further limitations will be placed upon private-member participation in enacting tax laws.

Budget debate

The British budget, it was noted in Chapter 5, is associated with the methods of the House for the raising of revenue. Debate on it, in the Committee of Ways and Means, is preliminary to the consideration of the Finance Bill. This procedure is difficult to defend in logic, for the budget relates as much to expenditure as it does to revenue. But more important than 'where', or 'when', the budget is debated in the House, is 'how'. There is clearly a need for a more systematic method to be devised for debate on a government's budget in a public assembly. A method is needed by which the annual financial plan—or even a plan for a longer period—may be considered as a whole and also by its component parts, and that the focus of the debate can be brought, in turn, on subjects such as monetary policy, trade policy, general fiscal policy, rate of growth, etc. A representative assembly in an advanced and industrialised society ought to be able to provide more than an innocuous and desultory discussion over two or three days wherein each speaker chases the last hare raised or rides his own hobby horse—or both. Western democracies have yet to come to grips with the incompatibilities of economic planning and the legislative power of popular assemblies. The procedural drift of the last century in matters of finance—usually explained in terms of tradition—is not enough. A great deal of experimentation is needed.

(ii) THE FINANCIAL SELECT COMMITTEES

In exercising their control via the three financial select committees (discussed in Chapter 4) members of the House of Commons have concentrated their interests almost wholly on matters of expenditure. Indeed, it is strange that financial control is often taken to mean 'expenditure control'. It has already been mentioned that the 'control' of revenue policy, or revenue raising, has not been delegated to select committees.

There is no quantitative measure of the contribution that the three existing select committees make towards expenditure control, or, generally speaking, what the House of Commons does to that end. Harold Wilson, for example, was despondent about the overall effect of the Public Accounts Committee and the Estimates Committee, when, as chairman of the former, he claimed—'These committees cannot do much, indeed the House cannot do much, to control the general volume of public expenditure.'[1] This presented a depressing picture for advocates of parliamentary democracy; and the situation is not significantly improved by the existence of the Select Committee on Nationalised Industries. But the accuracy of Wilson's statement depends completely upon what he meant by 'control'.

When public expenditure runs at the rate of over £7,000 millions annually, its details and all its social ramifications are beyond human comprehension. If control means the determination of spending priorities in any detail, and the allocation of fiscal resources to accord with assumptions about social utilities, it is obvious that Wilson is right—the three committees, as they function at present, 'cannot do much'. To be controllers in that sense the committees would need the assistance of large and informed secretariats to match, even to surpass, the expertise of the army of departmental officials who at present collate, even devise, the spending plans. Such control, however, would duplicate Executive effort; it would be wasteful and uneconomic; and it would threaten the power and the stability of government. It does not exist at present, and it is unlikely in the future.

But control by a representative assembly could mean simply the supervision of departmental expenditure to ensure that it accords with cash allocations formally made by the elected assembly after political debate. The purpose of that kind of control would be to

1. 650 HC Deb., 5s., c. 640.

ensure a degree of financial probity in public affairs. It is, of course, the basis of the present Gladstonian-control system, as designed and adapted over the last century; it continues to function and is reinforced by the work of the Comptroller and Auditor-General and the Select Committee of Public Accounts. The system is likely to prevail for many years yet, for financial rectitude in public affairs is a generally desirable endeavour in national politics. The British system of parliamentary appropriation and audit has been copied extensively, by democratic and non-democratic governments alike. But when, as in modern times, the representative body merely rubber-stamps the Executive's expenditure proposals (i.e. Estimates) the audit control as followed in Britain is, in effect, the Executive's method for the control of its own affairs in the name of Parliament. It is significant that in recent years Britain's Comptroller and Auditor-General (Sir Edmund Compton), in recognition of the limitations of audit control, has overtly sought higher justification for his existence. His objective has been to ensure that public business is conducted not only faithfully, but also economically. He has claimed that 'Methods of control need constant revision to match changes and developments in the subject matter of public expenditure'[1] and he has devised means to provide, through the work of his staff and the enquiries of the Public Accounts Committee, '. . . an incentive to efficiency, the counterpart perhaps in the Government field to the profit motive in the commercial field'.[2] This change of function was also acknowledged by Sir George Benson, who observed, after thirty years' service to the Public Accounts Committee, that its role '. . . had become not the rather narrow function of seeing whether expenditure and appropriation were analogous, but whether the departments were spending these sums efficiently and economically'.[3]

Does parliamentary control of finance then mean the provision by the representative body of incentives to efficiency? It is clear that such a goal would rank high, if not the highest, in the objectives of

1. Sir Edmund Compton, *op. cit.*, p. 17.
2. *ibid*, p. 14.   3. 632 H C Deb., 5s., c. 935.

the other two financial committees. The formal terms of reference of the Estimates Committee—to enquire whether policy 'implied' in the Estimates 'may be carried out more economically'—is, in fact, a caveat to the departments declaring that forty-three members of the House of Commons have a continuing interest in efficient administration, and will be searching each year for instances of uneconomic use of resources. And there is no doubt, that in the last two decades, the committee's enquiries have, on the whole, been biased in that direction.

But with the Select Committee on Nationalised Industries there is no declared interest in efficiency; indeed, such a declaration would exacerbate fears about parliamentary interference in industrial affairs beyond the jurisdiction of elected members. There is no doubt that the Committee's insistence upon the revelation by Ministers of their directives to the Boards of the relevant industries, is intended to have effects inseparable from theories of efficiency, based on the clarification of authority and responsibility. Moreover, numerous recommendations emerging through the committee's reports, referring to the control of stocks, depreciation policy, disposal of uneconomic coal pits, re-equipment of airlines, wagon turn-round in the railways, the importance of work study, are all quests for increased efficiency.

There is, therefore, a common thread in the functioning of the three select committees—it is their quest to secure an economic use of resources in the attainment of given political ends. But this is still vague, and it is not to deny Wilson's assertions that the committees 'cannot do much' to control public expenditure. The question is, how much check of this kind can seventy members make in the limited time they can spare each session. The influence these committees have on efficiency is, in fact, indirect, and even then it is based on limited enquiry. Collectively the enquiries undertaken amount to one nationalised industry per session, possibly a dozen subjects per year chosen by the Estimates Committee, and the few dozen issues that the Public Accounts Committee pursues after the annual audit report of the Comptroller and Auditor-General. The remainder of the enormous range of the activities of State are likely, in any one year, to remain unquestioned. Beyond the subjects examined directly, parliamentary financial control depends upon the latent sanctions that are inherent in possible enquiry, and in the possible revelation of waste and misuse of resources—it is, in the main, control by deterrent. For the political heads of the departments of State there is a continuing possibility of public embarrassment; and for civil servants a continuing possibility of career distortion. But it is clear that in existing conditions the purgative effect of financial control is on the whole a gentle one. The question of its optimum strength, and the dosage for a healthy body politic, calls for value judgements about how much discipline, restraint and interference is compatible with good government.

If parliamentary financial control, then, is a control based on policy debates in the whole House—restricted in their effect by procedural devices—plus the limited efficiency hunt, via the select committees, could it be said that parliamentary power is weakened by the division of the enquiring resources of the House of Commons into three select committees? Is this part of an Executive conspiracy to divide and rule? Would it be to the advantage of the House to consolidate its committee resources into one omnibus parliamentary organ for enquiry on a large scale? A union of the resources of the House in this respect would provide a committee of about seventy members, and by the use of sub-committees, and specialisation of effort, it could thus widen the scope and improve the opportunities for planned and integrated enquiry. The House could consolidate the existing staff of clerks into a single secretariat, and thereby develop for the committee an expertise in research appropriate to the tasks facing it. And, moreover, the change would aggregate the parliamentary authority of the three existing committees into one omniscient organ of expenditure (and possibly revenue) control.

There is no doubt that an omnibus committee would be compatible with the trend towards bigness in administration, including public administration, in modern times. It would provide a seemingly logical parliamentary counterpoise to the Leviathan Executive of the modern state. It would be the kind of development that Lord Haldane's 'Machinery of Government' Committee hinted at in 1918, when it 'adhered without reserve' to the view that:

It would, we think, be generally felt that any improvement in the organisation of the Departments of State which was so marked as substantially to increase their efficiency should have as its correlative an increase in the power of the Legislature as the check upon the acts and proposals of the Executive.[1]

The question of the unification of the financial committees was discussed before the Select Committee on Procedure in 1945–6. Sir Gilbert Campion (Clerk of the House) placed before that enquiry a plan for 'a comprehensive Committee on Public Expenditure . . . with an order of reference combining the functions of the Committee of Public Accounts and the Select Committee on Estimates'. He envisaged an organ for enquiry, at least thirty members strong, working through 'six investigating sub-committees', plus 'one co-ordinating sub-committee', to investigate finance over a three-year period: viz, the financial years, past, current and forthcoming. He wanted the committee divided into two divisions, corresponding to the two committees existing at the time, and the enquiries were to be based on the division of the accounts and estimates into four departmental groupings: (i) Defence Services, (ii) Treasury and Central Government, (iii) Trade, Industry and Transport, and (iv) Social Services. Campion expected 'that the knowledge and experience gained by the examination of accounts would be brought to bear on the examination of current expenditure and vice versa; and that a single committee would provide 'a method for co-ordinating the whole work of the examination of expenditure'.[2]

The 1945 proposal, however, met stiff opposition from the Labour Government. All manner of reasons were found to damn it, including:

1. Cd. 9230, p. 14.
2. HC 189–1 (Session 1945–6), pp. xx–xxv.

(i) The present committees can meet the modern requirements of Parliament far more effectively than Sir Gilbert Campion allows.

(ii) The Comptroller and Auditor-General and his staff could not possibly render advice and criticism over the whole field proposed 'much of which is quite alien to their statutory function . . .'.

(iii) The criteria applicable in an examination of audited accounts are quite different from those applicable to an examination of Estimates.

(iv) The demands of the committee would place a very heavy burden on senior officers and inevitably hamper efficiency of Executive action by importing delays and cramping initiative.

(v) The Rt Hon Herbert Morrison's opinion was that the committee would be 'a little bit liable to make civil servants lose their nerve' and that 'fellows in Whitehall' would think 'that there were some sleuths over at the Palace of Westminster running side by side with them trying to trip them up'.[1]

Although the Select Committee on Procedure reported in Campion's favour, the Government was adamant, and, lacking the back-bench support that the existing financial select committees had at their birth, the proposal lapsed.

Ironically, the twenty years since the rejection of the Campion proposal have shown the Government's decision to be to the House's advantage. With three financial select committees there is now a wider scope for independent enquiry, greater flexibility of action and more committee politics than members could have expected through one centralised body. The flexibility that each committee enjoys in the interpretation of its terms of reference injects an unpredictable quality into committee behaviour. It is more difficult for the Executive to control three committees than one omnibus body. In short, a centralisation of financial committee arrangements would lead to a countervailing centralisation of Executive restraints on select committee independence. If reform in the interest of the House is contemplated in the future, the advantages of the decentralised pattern of committee ought to be weighed heavily by back-bench members.

1. *ibid*, pp. 97–8, QQ. 3425 and 3470.

L

Indeed, a decentralised organisation of the House's financial committees was proposed to the Select Committee of Procedure in 1965. 'The Study of Parliament Group'—a private group of university teachers and officers of both Houses of Parliament (under the chairmanship of Sir Edward Fellowes, former Clerk of the House of Commons) —submitted a comprehensive plan for procedural reform, and three of its members gave evidence. The premise of their submission was that parliamentary 'control' meant 'influence, not direct power; advice, not command; criticism, not obstruction; scrutiny, not initiative, and publicity, not secrecy'. And to achieve that end they recommended three procedural reforms related to matters of finance, viz.:

(i) An increase in the size of the Estimates Committee so that more committees can 'review the expenditure of the main departments every year and that membership of these sub-committees should be subject to as little change as possible';

(ii) The creation of 'specialist committees', to work on lines similar to those of the Estimates Committee of Nationalised Industries Committee, to 'scrutinise the actions of government in their own fields, to collect, discuss and report evidence related to proceedings in Parliament, whether legislative or other'. As these committees are set up 'the Estimates Committee should devolve its relevant functions to them in their respective spheres'; and

(iii) the establishment of a Select Committee on Expenditure 'to explore the economic, factual and policy assumptions on which the forecast estimates had been prepared; to draw attention to the variations in the Estimates; and to examine their economic implications in terms of the availability of physical resources etc.'[1]

The Select Committee on Procedure considered the above suggestions and it took evidence and written submissions from officials of the House (including the Chairman of Ways and Means), the Head of the Civil Service, Ministers and ex-Ministers of the Crown, and back-benchers. Facing a wide range of proposals, both

1. HC 303 (Session 1964–5), appendix 2, pp. 131–42. The Group's witnesses were Professors P. A. Bromhead, A. H. Hanson, and H. Wiseman.

from witnesses and from its own members, it finally reported in favour of a modified Estimates Committee. It did not recommend an increased membership but it envisaged a new order of reference, viz.—'to examine how the departments of state carry out their responsibilities and to consider their Estimates of Expenditure and Reports'. The main change recommended was that the sub-committees of the Estimates Committee should develop special fields of interest, such as 'a sub-committee on social services'. In other words, it claimed that there should be a developing specialism in the work of the Committee—based on a questionable analogy with the Select Committee of Nationalised Industries.[1]

Once again, therefore, the case for strengthening the Committees of the House is being pressed. Again, a process of procedural politics is in train wherein forces are being marshalled and tactical manoeuvres executed for and against increasing the influence of the House vis-à-vis the Executive. Significant on this occasion, however, is the unusually forceful entry of an outside interest group pressing for reform, and also the stand of a back-bench individualist member of the committee who claimed that the idea of specialist committees 'is a delusion' and 'that the proliferation of parliamentary committees is not a cure but part of the disease'.[2] It remains to be seen whether, in the wider debate to follow, the issue will be called 'a House of Commons matter', whether the authority of 'the Constitution' will be imported in restraint of reform, whether 'the usual channels' will determine the decision to be taken, whether the Whip will be used, or whether back-benchers from both sides will display a readiness to unite against the front-benchers in the cause of reform.

The conclusion of this study, therefore, is somewhat paradoxical. Parliamentary control of finance although characterised by mythical qualities is not itself a myth. What mythical features there are, are devised to enable the Executive to cloak the degree of control it

1. The Leader of the House in 1965 (Rt. Hon. H. W. Bowden) finally left this question as 'a matter for the Estimates Committee' to determine. See 718 HC Deb., 5s., c. 185.
2. Mr Michael Foot, *ibid*, p. xiv. He was supported by former Conservative Chief Whip (Sir Martin Redmayne). And see 718 HC Deb., 5s., cc. 172–296.

exercises over the financial-legislative process in the elected assembly. The procedures for the Committee of Supply, the Committee of Ways and Means and Money Resolutions are usually explained in romantic terms (albeit suspect) about the Committees of the Whole House being a seventeenth-century device by which the House once escaped the influence of the King's man, the Speaker. As such they are procedures that have been 'ready', 'influential' and 'easy to get obeyed'. But, in reality, with the help of Rule 1, they each provide the means by which the legislative-financial power of the elective body may be held in check by the Executive; and in many respects the debating rules associated with them bolster the power of the party leaders over their rank and file. But it is to be noted that it is Rule 1, in its modern interpretation, that is the secret of the Executive's financial superiority. That rule is also explained in traditional terms to the effect that it is based on a Standing Order 'as old as the reign of Queen Anne', or it is accepted without question as 'a major constitutional principle'. But, be that as it may, the rule is now an arbitrary device used at the discretion of Ministers of the Crown—particularly since the reform of the franchise—enabling them to prescribe the degree of freedom in moving financial amendments that members of the House shall enjoy. And the rule can also be interpreted, in conditions of modern democracy, as an effective procedural restraint against threats to Britain's acquisitive society that are latent in an elective institution with legislative power.

But that is not to say that the Executive now controls the controllers, or that there is an Executive dictatorship in Parliament. As pointed out in Chapter 1, restrictions on debate are invoked on the initiative of front-benchers in a political context; and there have been countervailing pressures from back-benchers resisting limitations to their legislative freedom. And just as dictators must accept limitations upon their formal power so Ministers of the Crown, and leaders of political parties, frequently defer to the initiative and the resistance of members. Possibly it is trite, but there is enormous truth in the aphorism, that members of Parliament get the financial procedures, and the financial committees, they deserve.

SELECT BIBLIOGRAPHY

CHAPTER I. THE MYSTERIES OF PARLIAMENTARY FINANCIAL PROCEDURE

There are numerous studies, in varying degrees of technicality, of the origins of the procedures used in the House of Commons. For students of parliamentary method the more easily accessible, and most rewarding of these, are:

Anson, Sir W., *The Law and Custom of the Constitution* (fifth edition, OUP, 1922), vol I—Parliament.

Campion, Lord, *et al.*, *British Government since 1918* (Allen and Unwin, 1950), chapter I—Developments in the Parliamentary system since 1918 (by Lord Campion).

Campion, Lord, *et al.*, *Parliament: A survey* (Allen and Unwin, 1952), chapter 7—Parliamentary procedure—old and new (by Lord Campion).

Campion, Lord, *An introduction to the procedure of the House of Commons* (third edition, Macmillan, 1958), chapter I—Historical development of parliamentary procedure.

Einzig, Paul, *Control of the Purse* (Secker and Warburg, 1959).

Jennings, Sir I., *Parliament* (second edition, CUP, 1957), see chapter IX—Financial Control.

Mackenzie, K. R., *The English Parliaments* (Pelican, 1950).

May, T. Erskine, *Treatise on the Law, Privileges, Proceedings and Usages of*

Parliament (seventeenth edition, Butterworth, 1964). Edited by Sir Barnett Cocks. (Usually cited as Erskine May, *Parliamentary Practice*.) See particularly book I—Constitution, Powers and Privileges of Parliament. For details of financial procedures, see chapters XXVI to XXXI.

Redlich, J., *The Procedure of the House of Commons* (Constable, 1908). See book I—Historical; and see Preface written by Sir C. Ilbert (Clerk of the House of Commons 1902–21).

For a philosophical analysis of the procedures of deliberative assemblies, see:

Bentham, J., 'Essay on Political Tactics', in *The Works of Jeremy Bentham* (Tait, 1843), vol II, pp. 299–373.

For an early and pungent exposé of the front benches of the House of Commons as 'one close oligarchical corporation', see:

Belloc, H., and Chesterton, C., *The Party System* (Stephen Swift, 1911).

CHAPTER 2. CAMPION'S FOUR RULES OF FINANCIAL PROCEDURE

Campion's first exposition of the financial procedures of the House of Commons in terms of four 'rules' is to be found in the fourteenth (1946) and subsequent editions of Erskine May's *Parliamentary Practice*. In the seventeenth (1964) edition, see chapter XXVII—General Rules of Financia Procedure, pp. 713–34.

For studies of the financial methods, with explanations of their origins, see:

Anson, Sir W., *The Law and Custom of the Constitution, op. cit.*, chapter VI—The Process of Legislation.

Campion, Lord, *An introduction to the procedure of the House of Commons, op. cit.*, chapter VIII—Finance in the House of Commons.

Einzig, Paul, *Control of the Purse, op. cit.*, part One—Early Period; and part Two—Middle Period.

Redlich, J., *The Procedure of the House of Commons, op. cit.*, vol III, part XI—Financial Procedure.

Todd, Alpheus, *On Parliamentary Government in England; its origin, development and practical operation* (Spencer Walpole's edition, 1892), vol II, part IV—The Executive and Parliament, and part V—Parliament.

CHAPTER 3. THE CONTROL OF EXPENDITURE BY
PARLIAMENTARY DEBATE

Books

Campion, Lord, *An introduction to the procedure of the House of Commons,
op. cit.*, chapter VIII, pp. 257–85.

Davenport, E. H., *Parliament and the Taxpayer* (with an introduction by
Herbert Samuel) (Skeffington, 1918).

Hanson, A. H., *Parliament at Work* (Stevens and Sons, 1962), chapter IX—
Financial Procedure.

Hills, J. W., and Fellowes, E. A., *The Finance of Government* (second edition,
Philip Allen, 1932), chapter VIII—Public Economy.

Ilbert, Sir C., *Parliament: its history, constitution and practice* (Williams and
Northgate, London, 1911).

Jennings, Sir I., *Parliament, op. cit.*, chapter IX—Financial Control.

Low, Sir S., *The Governance of England* (revised edition, Unwin, 1914),
chapter V—The Control of Parliament.

Lowell, A. L., *The Government of England* (Macmillan, 1908), chapter XIV—
Procedure in the House of Commons.

May, T. Erskine, *Parliamentary Practice* (seventeenth edition, Butterworth,
1964), chapter XXVIII—Expenditure: Supply; and chapter XXIX—Expenditure: Money Resolutions.

Muir, R., *How England is Governed: A Critical Analysis of Modern Developments in the British System of Government* (second edition, Constable, 1930).

Redlich, J., *The Procedure of the House of Commons, op. cit.*, vol III, part XI—
Financial Procedure.

Taylor, E., *The House of Commons at Work* (fifth edition, Pelican, 1963),
chapter VI.

Young, E. Hilton (Lord Kennet), *The System of National Finance* (third
edition, Murray, 1936).

Articles and Pamphlets

Barker, A., 'Party and Supply', *Parliamentary Affairs*, vol XVII, no. 2
(Spring, 1964), pp. 207–17.

Barker, A., 'The Most Important and venerable function; a study of the
Commons' Supply procedure', *Political Studies*, vol XIII, no. 1 (February,
1965), pp. 45–64.

Caulcott, T. H., 'The Control of Public Expenditure', *Public Administration*, vol 40 (Autumn, 1962), pp. 267–88.

Fellowes, Sir E., 'Parliament and the Executive—Financial Control of the House of Commons', *Journal of the Parliaments of the Commonwealth*, vol XLIII (1962), pp. 223–31.

Tribe, Sir F., 'Parliamentary Control of Public Expenditure', *Public Administration*, vol XXXII (Winter, 1954), pp. 363–81.

Tribe, Sir F., 'The Control of Finance in Great Britain', *The Table* (the Journal of the Society of Clerks at the Table in Commonwealth Parliaments), vol XXVI (1957).

Walkland, S. A., 'The House of Commons and the Estimates, 1960', *Parliamentary Affairs*, vol XIII, no. 4 (Autumn, 1960), pp. 477–88.

Parliamentary Supply Procedure, H.M. Treasury Booklet, 1953.

There is a wealth of material relevant to the development of parliamentary control of expenditure in the reports of the numerous select committees of the House of Commons appointed to enquire into procedural issues. The relevant reports are:

1857	*Select Committee on Public Moneys*, HC 279 of 1857 (Session 2 vol IX).
	Select Committee on the Conduct of Public Business in the Committee of Supply, HC 261 of 1857 (Session 2, vol IX).
1888	*Select Committee on Estimates Procedure*, HC 281 of 1888 (vol XII).
1902	*Select Committee on National Expenditure*, HC 387 of 1902 (vol VII) and HC 243 of 1903 (vol VII).
1914	*Select Committee on Procedure*, HC 378 of 1914 (vol VII).
1918	*Select Committee on National Expenditure—Ninth Report*, HC 121 of 1918 (vol IV).
1931–2	*Select Committee on Procedure*, HC 129 of 1931–2 (vol V).
1936–7	*Select Committee on Money Resolutions*, HC 149 of 1936–7 (vol VIII).
1945–6	*Select Committee on Procedure—Third Report*, HC 189–1 of 1945–6 (vol IX).
1956–7	*Select Committee on Procedure—First Report*, HC 100 of 1956–7.
1958–9	*Select Committee on Procedure*, HC 92–1 of 1958–9.

1962–3 Select Committee on Procedure—Third Report, HC 271 of 1962–3.

1964–5 Select Committee on Procedure—Fourth Report, HC 303 of 1964–5.

For some wider enquiries into Treasury Control, and into Treasury and parliamentary relationships with the Comptroller and Auditor-General, see:

Beer, S. H., *Treasury Control. The co-ordination of financial and economic policy in Great Britain* (OUP, 1956).

Bridges, Lord, *The Treasury* (Allen and Unwin, 1964).

Brittain, Sir Herbert, *The British Budgetary System* (Allen and Unwin, 1959).

Brittan, Samuel, *The Treasury under the Tories, 1951–1964* (Penguin, 1965).

Compton, Sir E., *Control of Public Expenditure* (The Institute of Municipal Treasurers and Accountants, 1960).

Durell, A. J. V., *The Principles and Practice of the System of Control over Parliamentary Grants* (Hogg, 1917).

Hawtrey, Sir R., *The Exchequer and the Control of Expendure* (London, 1921).

Hicks, J. R., *The Problem of Budgetary Reform* (OUP, 1948).

Hicks, Ursula K., *British Public Finances, 1880–1952* (OUP), 1954.

Higgs, Henry, *Financial Reform* (Macmillan, 1924).

Peacock, A. T., and Robertson, D. J. (eds.), *Public Expenditure—Appraisal and Control* (Oliver and Boyd, 1963).

Final Report of the Committee on the Form of Government Accounts (Crick Committee), Cmd 7969 (1950).

Treasury Control of Expenditure (Sixth Report from the Select Committee on Estimates), HC 254–1 (Session 1957–8).

Control of Public Expenditure (Plowden Report), Cmnd 1432 (1961).

Reform of the Exchequer Accounts, Cmnd 2014 (1963).

Treasury Control of Establishments (Fifth Report from the Estimates Committee), HC 228 (Session 1963–4).

Third Report from the Estimates Committee—Form of the Estimates, HC 184 (Session 1960–1).

Second Report from the Estimates Committee—The form of the Civil Supplementary Estimates, HC 41 (Session 1962–3).

Sixth Report from the Estimates Committee—The timing of the presentation of Supplementary Estimates, HC 228 (Session 1962–3).

CHAPTER 4. THE FINANCIAL SELECT COMMITTEES

There is an increasing volume of literature on the House's financial control by Select Committees. For an overall view of committee activity in this field, see:

Chubb, B., *The Control of Public Expenditure* (OUP, 1952).

Crick, B., *The Reform of Parliament* (Weidenfeld and Nicolson, 1964), see chapter 4—What the Commons do collectively.

Hill, A., and Whichelow, A., *What's Wrong with Parliament?* (Penguin, 1964), chapter 5—Committees to Advise and Recommend.

Wheare, K. C., *Government by Committee* (OUP, 1955), chapter VIII—Committees to Scrutinise and Control.

For consideration of specific committees, see:

Public Accounts Committee

Chubb, B., *The Control of Public Expenditure*, op. cit., chapter VII—The Public Accounts Committee.

Einzig, Paul, *Control of the Purse*, op. cit., chapter 27—The Public Accounts Committee.

Wilson, H., 'The Control of public expenditure', *The Guardian* (London) (Friday, 21 October 1960).

Estimates Committee

Chubb, B., *The Control of Public Expenditure*, op. cit., chapter VIII—The Estimates Committee 1912–14 and 1921–9, and chapter IX—The National Expenditure Committee and the present Estimates Committee.

Einzig, Paul, *Control of the Purse*, op. cit., chapter 30—The Select Committee on Estimates.

Miller, B., 'The Colonial Office and the Estimates Committee', *Public Administration*, vol 39 (Summer, 1961), pp. 173–9.

Nicholson, Sir G., 'The Colonial Office and the Estimates Committee', *Public Administration*, vol 40 (Summer, 1962), pp. 151–7.

Select Committee on Nationalised Industries

Chester, D. N., 'Boards and Parliament', *Public Administration*, vol XXXVI (Spring, 1958), pp. 87–92.

Coombs, D., 'The Scrutiny of Ministers' powers by the Select Committee on Nationalised Industries', *Public Law* (Spring, 1965), pp. 9–29.

Daniel, G. N., 'Public Accountability of the Nationalised Industries', *Public Administration*, vol XXXVIII (Spring, 1960), pp. 27–34.

Goodhart, A. L., 'Parliamentary control over the Nationalised Undertakings' in Lord Campion *et al.*, *Parliament—A Survey, op. cit.*, pp. 252–71.

Grove, J., 'British Public Corporations: Some recent developments', *Journal of Politics*, vol 18 (1956), pp. 651–77.

Hanson, A. H., 'Parliamentary questions on the nationalised industries', *Public Administration*, vol XXIX (Spring, 1951), pp. 51–66.

Hanson, A. H., 'Parliamentary Control of Nationalised Industries', *Parliamentary Affairs*, vol XI, no. 3 (Summer, 1958), pp. 328–40.

Hanson, A. H. (ed.), *Nationalisation: A Book of Readings* (Allen and Unwin, 1963), chapter VII—Parliament and the Enterprise.

Johnson, E. L., 'Accountability of British Nationalised Industries', *American Political Science Review*, vol XLVIII (June, 1954), pp. 366–85.

Low, Sir T., 'The Select Committee on Nationalised Industries', *Public Administration*, vol 40 (Spring, 1962), pp. 1–15.

Morrison, Lord, *Government and Parliament: A Survey from the Inside* (OUP, 1954), chapter XII—Socialisation of Industry: Public Control and Accountability.

Robson, W. A., *Nationalised Industries and Public Ownership* (Allen and Unwin, 1960), chapters VI, VII and VIII. (And see Professor Robson's 'Select Bibliography', *ibid*, pp. 513–15.)

CHAPTER 5. RAISING THE REVENUE

Less has been written about the House of Commons' control of revenue than about its control of expenditure. For explanations of its methods, and their origins, see:

Bowles v. Bank of England. The Proceedings and Official Court Documents (Butterworth, 1914).

Bridges, Lord, *The Treasury, op cit.*, part Three—Finance; and part Four—Economic Co-ordination.

Brittain, Sir Herbert, *The British Budgetary System, op. cit.*, chapters I to IX.

Campion, Lord, *An introduction to the procedure of the House of Commons, op. cit.*, chapter VIII—Finance in the House of Commons.

Crombie, Sir ⸳., *Her Majesty's Customs and Excise* (Allen and Unwin, 1962).

Dicey, A. V., *Introduction to the study of the Law of the Constitution* (Macmillan, 1885), chapter x—The Revenue.

Jennings, Sir I., *Parliament, op. cit.*, chapter ix—Financial Control.

Keeton, G. W., *The Passing of Parliament* (Benn, 1952), chapter 9—Taxation and Freedom.

May, T. Erskine, *Parliamentary Practice* (seventeenth edition, 1964), *op. cit.*, chapter xxx—Ways and Means.

For some recent enquiries into the House's scrutiny of the Annual Finance Bill, see:

Report from the Select Committee on Procedure, HC 92–1 (Session 1958–9), pp. viii–xi.

Second Report from the Select Committee on Procedure—Expediting the Finance Bill, HC 190 (Session 1962–3).

Third Report from the Select Committee on Procedure, HC 276 (Session 1964–5).

CHAPTER 6. IS PARLIAMENTARY FINANCIAL CONTROL A MYTH?

For some contemporary enquiries into 'parliamentary reform', see:

Bromhead, P., 'How should Parliament be Reformed?', *Political Quarterly*, vol xxx, no. 3 (1959), pp. 272–82.

Brown, Sir W., *et al.*, *Change or Decay: Parliament and Government in an Industrial Society* (Conservative Political Centre, 1963).

Crick, B., *Reform of the Commons* (Fabian Tract 319, 1959).

Foot, M., *Parliament in Danger* (Pall Mall, 1959).

Hanson, A. H., 'The Purpose of Parliament', *Parliamentary Affairs*, vol xvii, no. 3 (Summer, 1964), pp. 279–95.

Hill, A., and Whichelow, A., *What's Wrong with Parliament?*, *op. cit.*

Hollis, C., *Can Parliament Survive?* (Hollis and Carter, 1949).

Jennings, Sir I., *Parliamentary Reform* (Gollancz, 1934).

Jennings, Sir I., *Parliament Must be Reformed* (Kegan Paul, 1941).

Parliamentary Reform, 1933–60: A Survey of suggested reforms (Cassell, 1961).

Political Quarterly (Special Number on Parliament), vol 36, no. 3 (July–September 1965).

Wiseman, H. V., 'Parliamentary Reform', *Parliamentary Affairs*, vol xii, no. 2 (1959), pp. 240–54.

INDEX

'ALLOTTED' DAYS (for Supply debates), 73–4, 79, 150
Anne, Queen, 44
Anson, Sir William, 41, 44, 77
Appropriation, 36, 52–8, 78, 157
Asquith, H. H., 96–7
Assheton, R., 106
Attlee, Lord, 83, 88–9
Australia:
    Constitution, 42–3
    House of Representatives, 11
Ayrton, C. J., 40–1, 49

BACKBENCHERS:
    Finance Bill, 142–3
    influence on financial select committees, 93–8, 108
    versus frontbenchers, 28, 29, 44, 80, 127, 133, 163
Bagehot, W., 15, 18, 31, 35, 41, 49, 63, 68
Baldwin, S., 85, 135
Balfour, A. J., 23, 69–70, 73
Barber, A., 111
Barker, Sir Ernest, 14
Benson, Sir George, 105, 157
Bentham, J., 14, 60–1, 148
Bevan, A., 89, 130
Bill of Rights, 17, 36, 53
Borrowing, 128–9
Bowles, T. Gibson, 135
Boyd-Carpenter, J., 107
Bradlaugh v. Gossett, 17, 21
Bridges, Lord, 82, 114
British North America Act (1867), 42
Brooke, H., 43–4, 65
Budget:
    'amendment of the law' resolution, 137, 140–1

J. Morley's definition, 130
procedures for, 130–47, reform of, 155
Burke, E., 18
Butler, R. A., 17, 24, 71, 86, 91, 110, 113, 118–19

CAMPBELL-BANNERMAN, Sir Henry, 23
Campion, Lord, 18, 20, 32–4, 46, 54, 67, 149, 153–4, 160
    Finance Bill, 139
    four rules of financial procedure, 33–61, 128, 131, 149
    money resolutions, 85, 153–4
    plan for Committee on Public Expenditure, 160–2
Canada, 42
    Public Accounts Committee, 95
Carr, R., 111
Charles I, 128
Charles II, 46, 48
Chubb, B., 57fn, 94
Civil Contingencies Fund, 82–3
    Closure (Cloture), 22
    on Consolidated Fund Bills, 80
Collectivism, effect on procedures, 66–7
Committee of the Whole House:
    legislation in, 78
Committees of the Whole House—
    the preliminary consideration of financial proposals in (Rule 2), 16, 34, 45–52, 60, 63–4, 73, 81, 84–92
    Committee of Ways and Means, 75–7, 133–47
    money resolutions, 84–92
    Provisional Collection of Taxes Act (1913), 136
    Supply business, 64–75, 75–7
    taxation business, 133–47

Comptroller and Auditor-General, 10, 58, 76, 83, 114–15, 150, 157
  guided missile contracts, 112
  relevance to Select Committees on Estimates and Nationalised Industries, 117–19
Conservatism, influence on procedure, 15, 18, 99
Conservative Party:
  Chairman of Nationalised Industries Committee, 107
  members on Public Accounts Committee, 105
  1922 Committee, 99
Consolidated Fund, 75
Consolidated Fund Acts (or Bills):
  authorising new services by, 80
  Consolidated Fund (Appropriation) Bill, 78, 82
  procedure for, 77–9, 81
Consolidated Fund Services, 64
Constitution:
  and parliamentary procedure, 15, 30, 76
  revenue raising, 127, 142
Control (see Financial Control)
Cornewell Lewis, Sir Edward, Ruling on money resolutions, 87
Crick, B., 94, 98fn, 153–4
'Crick' Committee, report 'The Form of Public Accounts', 11, 12, 115
Cripps, Sir Stafford, 140
Cross, R., 107
Crossman, R. H. S., 41
Customs and Inland Revenue Bill (later Finance Bill), 138

DEFENCE ESTIMATES (see Estimates of Expenditure)
Denison, Mr Speaker, 39–40
Derby, Lord, 39–40, 48
Dicey, A. V., 66–8
Disraeli, B., 39–40
Durham, Lord, 42

EDEN, SIR ANTHONY, 113
Edward III, 56
Einzig, P., 57fn, 71–2, 94, 133
Eliot, Sir John, 46, 73
Estimates Committee, 29, 93–126, 156–8
  chairman, 102–3, 106–7
  enquiries into policy, 122–6
  expert assistance, 114–22
  influence on debates, 72, 80
  membership, 102, 104–8, 115
  origin, 29
  reports, 103–4, 109–14; on Treasury Control, 11, 80

Estimates of Expenditure, 52, 58, 64–5, 68–71, 75, 84, 116–17
  debates on, 149–53
  Defence Estimates, 65, 81
  'Examiner' of, 115
  financial control by, 157
  preparation of, 80
  Revised Estimates, 81
  (and see Supply, Committee of)
Excess Grant, 65, 81
Exchequer and Audit Department Act (1866), 76, 95
Exchequer, Report—'Reform of Exchequer Account', 12, 84
Expenditure commitments, control of, 152–3

FELLOWES, SIR EDWARD, 62–3, 77, 133fn
Finance Bill, 99, 127–45, 147
  Committal to standing Committee, 142–3
Financial Committees (see Public Accounts, Estimates, Nationalised Industries)
Financial Control, definitions, 10, 152–3, 156–7, 162
Financial Initiative of the Crown (Rule 1), 30–1, 34, 35–45, 65, 67, 81, 89, 164
  money resolutions, 84–92
  supply business, 65–9
  taxation business, 131–3
Fitzroy, Mr Speaker, 88
Frontbenchers, 44, 72, 142–3

GAITSKELL, H., 19, 106
Gladstone, W. E., 22, 39, 40, 130
Gladstonian system of accounts, 10, 58, 66, 95, 97, 121, 130, 138, 151, 157
Goldsmid, Sir H. d'Avigdor, 111
Gossett, H. (see Bradlaugh v. Gossett)
Griffith, J. A. G., 148
Guided missiles, Public Accounts Committee reports, 112–13
Guillotine procedure, 70

'HALDANE' REPORT (1918), 160
Hale, L., 75
Hatsell, J., 14, 33, 37, 48, 59, 134
Hawtrey, Sir Ralph, 32, 76
Henry IV, 55
Henry VIII, 54
Hinchingbrooke, Lord, 124
  'revolt', 71, 74–5, 110
Hooker, J., 59
Houghton, D., 106
Hume, J., 38, 68, 70

ILBERT, SIR COURTENAY, 16, 87, 148
Import Duties Act (1958), 128

JENNINGS, SIR IVOR, 77, 148

KENNET, LORD (E. HILTON YOUNG),
62-3

LASKI, H., 31-2, 97-8, 115-17
Leader of the House, 26, 74
Lees-Smith, W., 88-9
Legislation:
    ability of members to amend, 89
    role of the House of Commons, 146-55
    (and see Money resolutions)
Legislation—authorisation of financial
    charges by (Rule 3), 34, 52-8, 62-3,
    81, 146-9
    ex Supply business, 77-9
    ex Ways and Means business, 138-45
Lidderdale, D. W. S., 151fn
Litchfield, J., 104
Lloyd George, D., 89, 96
    Budget (1909,) 99, 135-6
Lords, House of, 53, 54-6, 64
    relations with House of Commons,
    99-100
Low, Sir Toby, 108, 119
Lowther, Mr Speaker, 86

MACLEOD, I., 25, 124
Macmillan, H., 19, 23-4
Magna Carta, 35
May, Sir T. Erskine, 22, 33, 36, 37-8, 51,
    57fn, 64, 68, 72, 77, 80, 132, 135
Mill, J. S., 41, 147-8
Milman, A. J., 69
Molson, H., 97-8, 100, 107-8, 113
'Money' Committees, 47, 50, 84-92
Money resolutions, 52, 84-92, 146
    reform, 153-4
Morley, J., 130
Morrison, Lord, 23
Morrison, Mr Speaker, 73
Muir, R., 133

NABARRO, G., 75fn
National Expenditure—Select Committees
    on, 97
National Loans Act (1939), 129
Nationalised Industries, Select Committee
    on, 72, 93-126, 158
    chairman, 102-3, 106-7
    enquiries into policy, 122-6
    expert assistance for, 114-22
    membership, 102, 104-8
    origin, 29, 97-9
    reports, 103-4, 109-14

New expenditure services:
    approval, 80
    control of commitments, 152-3
Nicholson, Sir Godfrey, 108, 111-12,
    116fn, 122fn
Notestein, W., 45-6

OPPOSITION, THE, 26, 45
    'allotted' days, 73-4, 150

PADMORE, SIR THOMAS, 106
Palgrave, Sir Reginald, 33, 68fn
Pannell, C., 25, 27fn
Paper Duties Repeal Bill (1860), 99
Parliament Acts, the (1911 and 1949), 9,
    21, 36, 99-100
Parties, 44, 127
    discipline, 52
Patten, W., 39
Peake, O., 106, 115, 122fn
Petition of Grievance, 36
Petition of Right, 36
Petitions, 36-7
Pickthorn, Sir Kenneth, 30
Plowden Committee, Report—'Control of
    Public Expenditure', 11, 151-2
Policy bills, approval of financial clauses,
    84-92
Politics, restraint of, 72
Procedure:
    conservatism, 15, 18, 99
    definitions, 13, 14
    'dignified', 75
    'House of Commons' matter, 22, 24,
    127, 163
    procedural politics, 20, 27-8, 44, 75
    reform, 146-64
    select committees on—
        1857, 75
        1861, 17
        1888, 68-9
        1902-3, 71, 96
        1918, 71, 115
        1930-1, 115
        1931-2, 71
        1936-7, 43, 89-90
        1945-6, 71, 73, 115
        1948, 12-13
        1952-3, 98
        1955-6, 98-9
        1956-7, 91
        1958-9, 71, 73, 91, 142
        1962-3, 142, 148
        1964-5, 91-2
Provisional Collection of Taxes Act
    (1913), 21, 136

Public Accounts and Charges Act (1891), 21
Public Accounts Committee, 58, 93–126, 156–7
  chairman, 102–3, 106–7
  enquiries into policy, 122–6
  expert assistance for, 114–22
  membership, 102, 104–8
  origin, 29, 94–6
  reports, 103–4, 109–14, on guided missile contracts, 112–13, 123
Public Expenditure Committee, Lord Campion's proposal, 160–2
Purchase Tax, 128, 140–1

QUEEN, SPEECH FROM THE THRONE, 64

REDLICH, J., 22, 61, 64
Reform Bill (1866) (Gladstone's), 40
Reith, Lord, 125
Revenue business, procedures for, 127–45
Revised Estimates, 65, 81
Runciman, W., 27

SAMUEL, H., 115
Scobell, H., 46
Select Committees (see Procedure—Select Committees on, and see Estimates, Public Accounts and Nationalised Industries)
Shaw-Lefevre, Mr Speaker, 38
Silverman, S., 75
Smith, Adam, 57
Somerville, Sir Donald, 89
Speaker, Mr:
  nominee of Crown, 50
  procedural questions, 45, 50, 86–7, 90
  spokesman for House, 55
Standing Committees (for legislation), 78
Standing Orders:
  financial select committees, 63fn, 102
  general, 1–32
Statutum de Tallagio non Concedendo, 35, 36
Supplementary Estimates, 65, 81, 83–4, 150
  spring, summer, winter Supplementary Estimates, 81
  Supplementary Estimates on Account, 81
Supply, Committee of, 47, 52, 58, 64–75, 76, 146
  'allotted' days, 69–74
  nexus with Committee of Ways and Means, 134
  reform, 149–53
  restrictive procedures in, 79, 83–4 (and see Estimates of Expenditure)
'Supply' expenditure, definition of, 85

TARIFF, 128
Taxation, 11, 52, 128
  'amendment of the law' resolution, 137, 140–1
  procedures for, 46, 127–45
  reform of procedures, 154–5 (and see Ways and Means, etc.)
Taylor, E., 79fn
Tennyson, Lord, 19
Time-intervals between stages of financial business (Rule 4), 49, 58–61
  Consolidated Fund Bills, 79
  Finance Bills, 136, 144–5
Todd, A., 75–6, 132
Touche, Sir Gordon, 78
Treasury, 80, 82–3, 86, 128, 142
  official to help Estimates Committee, 115
Treasury control, 65
Tribe, Sir Frank, 124

UNEMPLOYMENT INSURANCE BILL (1922): ruling re money resolution, 87
Union, Act of (Canada), 42
'Usual Channels', 25, 74, 143

VIREMENT, 82
Vote on Account, 65, 81

WANT OF CONFIDENCE MOTIONS:
  interpretation of financial questions as, 75
Waterhouse, C., 107
Ways and Means, Committee of, 47, 52, 75, 127–46
  'amendment of the law' resolution, 137, 140–1
  budget debate, 133–8, 155
  Chairman of, 138, power of selecting amendments on Finance Bill, 141–3
  Provisional Collection of Taxes Bill (1913), effects, 136
  reform, 154–5
  rendered a façade, 137
  'spending' function, 75–7, 81
Webb, S., 87
Westminster Model, 11, 42, 45, 72fn
Wheare, Sir Kenneth, 30–1, 94
Whip, use of in procedural matters, 24–5, 27fn, 52, 78, 163
White Fish and Herring Industry Bill (1961), 92
Wilson, H., 27fn, 105–6, 108, 110–2, 123, 156

YOUNG, E. HILTON (see Kennet, Lord)